# A PERFECTLY GOOD

# GUITAR

BRAD AND MICHELE MOORE ROOTS MUSIC SERIES

# A PERFECTLY GOOD

# GUITAR

### ● MUSICIANS ON THEIR FAVORITE INSTRUMENTS ●

—

## CHUCK HOLLEY

UNIVERSITY OF TEXAS PRESS, AUSTIN

The publication of this book was made possible by the generous support of Ellen and Ed Randall. Their donation is dedicated to their daughter Helen Randall, in appreciation of many happy memories.

Requests for permission to reproduce material
from this work should be sent to:
    Permissions
    University of Texas Press
    P.O. Box 7819
    Austin, TX 78713-7819
    http://utpress.utexas.edu/index.php/rp-form

The paper used in this book meets the minimum requirements
of ANSI/NISO Z39.48-1992 (R1997) (Permanence of Paper). ∞

LIBRARY OF CONGRESS CATALOGING-IN-PUBLICATION DATA

Names: Holley, Chuck, author.
Title: A perfectly good guitar / Chuck Holley.
Other titles: Brad and Michele Moore roots music series.
Description: Austin : University of Texas Press, 2017. |
    Series: Brad and Michele Moore roots music series
Identifiers: LCCN 2016030561 | ISBN 978-1-4773-1257-5
    (cloth : alk. paper) | ISBN 978-1-4773-1258-2 (library e-book) |
    ISBN 978-1-4773-1259-9 (non-library e-book)
Subjects: LCSH: Guitar. | Guitarists—United States.
Classification: LCC ML1015.G9 H67 2017 | DDC 787.87/19—dc23
LC record available at https://lccn.loc.gov/2016030561

doi:10.7560/312575

# CONTENTS

# INTRODUCTION

I HAVE ALWAYS LIKED photography, music, and a good story. Those three things came together on a summer evening in 2007 at Island Park in Cedar Falls, Iowa.

Puddin' Truck, a local band, was playing at The Beach House on a Saturday night. I stayed until the bitter end, chatting with the band as I finished my beer. Rick Oltman, a guitarist, was packing up his rig when I struck up a conversation.

"You sounded good tonight, but I couldn't help but notice the wear on your guitar," I said. "What happened?"

What followed was an account of his experiences beginning with the day he purchased the guitar.

Rick was eighteen years old in 1969, living in Waterloo, Iowa. With his parents' permission, he withdrew four hundred dollars from his savings account and boarded a Greyhound bus bound for Minnesota in January. He was in search of a guitar.

He purchased a 1969 Gibson Les Paul with a Kustom amp head from B Sharp Music in Minneapolis for $444.44. The guitar was nearly stolen at the bus terminal as Rick waited to return home . . . the first, but not the last, time that there would be a story he could tell about his guitar.

In the mid-1970s, he was playing with a band in Effingham, Illinois. After a performance one night, he set his Les Paul on the guitar stand next to the jukebox where he thought it would be out of the way. It was, until an inebriated woman bumped into the juke-box and fell into the guitar, bending the bridge.

The next day, he removed the bridge with a screwdriver. "I didn't have a car, so I stuck this bent bridge in my pocket and started walking," said Rick. "I walked through this rough industrial town until I found a machine shop."

After explaining his problem to the machinist, he watched as the bridge was placed in a vise where it was bent, tugged, and pounded to the shape resembling the original arc. He reattached it, and there it remained on his Les Paul until he got around to replacing it years later.

A few weeks later, I thought about my conversation with Rick. There are lots of things to which people assign value. A piece of jewelry can be worth more to someone than any appraised value. A memento, a reminder of another time, can hold value, real or perceived. That includes guitars. There must be other players with their own stories. All I had to do was ask.

I began an eight-year search, looking for professional guitarists who would be willing to recall how they acquired that one special instrument and why it grew in importance to them.

I've heard about both acoustic and electric guitars. With a few notable exceptions, the vast majority are commercially made. I held no allegiance to a particular brand. Some were made by the finest luthiers while others were assembled from parts. Perhaps the oddest conversation centered on cigar box guitars.

At the outset, I envisioned a collection of stories about six-string guitars. Not basses, mandolins, banjos, or pedal steel guitars. I didn't have many parameters, but I felt I should have some.

Those parameters were challenged in my first conversation with Nashville player James Pennebaker.

I found James to be a nice guy, ready to share his story about an early Fender lap steel. I wanted to hear his tale, but I explained my interest was in six-string guitars.

James is something of an instrument historian. He explained that the lap steel guitar is the direct forerunner of the solid body electric guitar. If it were not for the lap steel, it's possible that Leo Fender never would have developed his first solid body electric guitar, marketed as the Fender Broadcaster. The Broadcaster gave way to the "Nocaster." Production of the Telecaster followed, and Fender later introduced the Stratocaster. Both models, to this day, are staples in the industry.

So James took me to school, and that education led me to stories from Cindy Cashdollar and Greg Leisz. James also had a damned good story. For that, I am grateful to him.

I interviewed dozens of professionals, and most of the artists I approached were quite willing to visit with me. I'm grateful to all who were gracious enough to discuss their guitar of choice.

The instrument represents different things to different people. To some, it's nothing more than a tool. To others, it can represent something more. A guitar can be special because of how it was acquired. Perhaps it's a gem discovered in a pawnshop—a diamond in the rough taken home, polished, and given a new life. Everyone likes a bargain, but in the age of the Internet, eBay, and Craigslist, the pawnshop bargains are almost a thing of the past.

A guitar can be a tool for healing both debilitating physical setbacks and emotional scars. It can heal the body and the soul—a tool most likely overlooked by modern medicine.

Guitars come and go. Some artists continually buy and sell guitars in a search for the Holy Grail, that one "perfect" guitar. And the ingredients for that perfection begin with the wood chosen for the body. The stain, the radius of the neck, the fingerboard, the strings, the bridge, the saddle, the pickups, and the action all determine how it sounds to the discerning ear. These elements meld, like a gumbo, to form the perfect guitar. However, perfection for one artist could be all but unplayable for another.

Some artists part with a guitar out of necessity. As one put it:

> For the most part, people buy an instrument because they are flirting with the love of playing music. It's the beginning of dreams. At the time you buy a guitar, there is an entire lifetime of dreams which flash before them.
>
> They say, "I'm going to play guitar!" Ninety-nine percent of the time that doesn't happen. But that doesn't matter. Guitars embody a lot of dreams.

Selling a guitar is, for the most part, a feeling of failure.

They may say, "I didn't learn it or I need the money." The last thing anyone wants to do is sell a guitar. It symbolizes a closure and moving on from a dream. It's not a good time.

As one songwriter put it, he doesn't hesitate to sell a guitar if he's not using it. Sometimes, as a result of an unforgiving business, the money beckons. The need to eat remains and the guitar becomes a currency reluctantly passed on to the next guardian. That begs the question: does anyone really own a guitar or are they caretakers for the next person?

From the beginning, my interest was in talking with working professionals. Some are better known to the public than others. All are respected by their peers. Some can play scorching licks while others display more limited skills. "I'm not a great guitar player," admitted Rosanne Cash. Cornell Hurd said, "I play rhythm guitar in my band. It's all shuffles and boogie-woogie. I'm a one-trick pony; my job is to entertain people and run the band."

Both Cash and Hurd acknowledge that their guitar skills are on a different level when compared to other players. Yet, both are songwriters with important roles in their bands. I've collected stories from players who are among the best in their field. But the tool used by the songwriters, who may not be technically great players, is the same.

This is not a book of lists. It doesn't represent any sort of ranking; there are plenty of books that already do that. Nor is this in any way comprehensive. There are a lot of people in this world who play. Instead, this is a collection of stories from some talented musicians. The element common to all their stories is the one tool they all use—the guitar.

# A PERFECTLY GOOD

## GUITAR

# DAVE ALVIN

## A NATIONAL STEEL AMONG THE HOPI DOLLS

Most great things in life come your way when you don't go looking for them. A tribal art show isn't the kind of place where you'd normally look for a 1934 National Steel Body Resonator guitar. So, in a way, it made total sense that it would be there.

I started accumulating guitars when I was in the Blasters. When I started my solo career, this little need called "money" popped up. I wasn't generating as much money as I was making in either the Blasters or X, so I had to a sell a bunch of guitars.

I had a 1964 Fender Mustang and a '64 Strat. Those were sacrosanct. I had a guitar that had belonged to Johnny Cash. It was a Fender acoustic, and it had his name in mother of pearl on the neck. There was an Everly Brothers guitar and a John Lennon Gibson. I had a Fender baritone guitar and a dogged-up '61 Strat. Except for that '64 Fender and the '64 Strat, I had to sell all of them.

When I started making money again in the early '90s, I decided I'm not gonna buy guitars because I'll just have to sell them. What I wanted were a couple of great acoustics and a couple of great electrics. I had always wanted a great National Steel, but I didn't go out of my way to look for it.

Anyway, I'm not really a guitar collector. One thing I do collect is antique Native American art. Specifically, Southwest stuff—Navajo rugs, Pueblo pottery, Hopi kachina dolls. In 2001, I was at an art show in LA that specializes in tribal art. I was just walking around and I spotted this 1934 National Steel Resonator Duolian guitar in

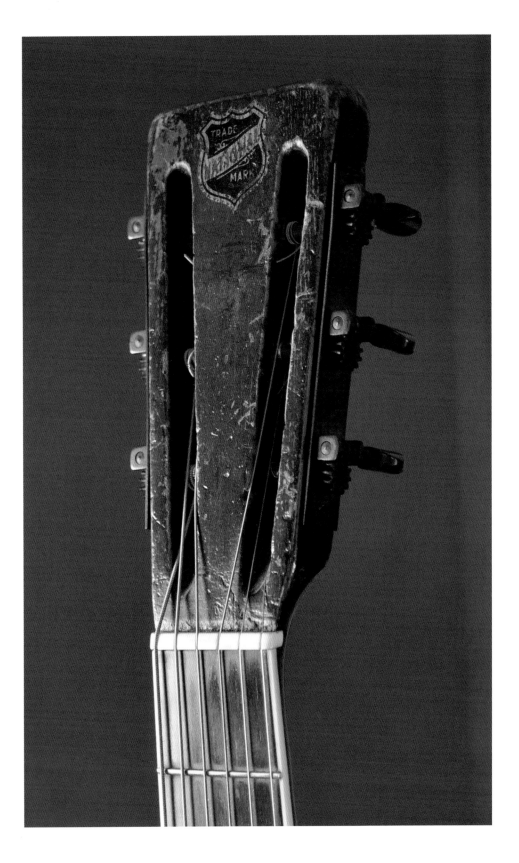

one of the booths. I made a beeline for it. I asked the guy if I could look at it. It's not made for slide, although you can play slide on it. It has a big, rounded neck, not a square slide neck. It's a picking guitar with an art deco palm design on it. It was love at first touch.

We were talking about the guitar and going back and forth as guys do. Finally, he looks at me and says, "You're one of the Alvins, aren't you?"

I said, "Yeah."

"I got high with your brother a few years back."

I said, "Well, then, do you want to sell the guitar?"

He said $1,500 and it's yours. I didn't have the money, so I wrote a check for $750, gave him my address, and left with the guitar. A couple of weeks later, I paid him the rest.

This is a great guitar. I've used it on a couple of albums, but I tend not to record with it that much. I haven't written a song that's a showcase for it yet. But I just made a record with my brother, Phil, called *Common Ground* and it's all over that thing. And I recorded a version of an old Johnny Dodds instrumental called "Perdido Street Blues." It's only available online, but I'll release it someday.

My friend Greg Leisz played it one day, and he looked at me and said, "You're not good enough to have this guitar." He's probably right.

DAVE ALVIN spent his youth sneaking into blues bars with his older brother, Phil, to see and learn from masters like Big Joe Turner, T-Bone Walker, and Lightning Hopkins. He quit his day job as a fry cook in 1979 when he and Phil formed the seminal roots rock band, the Blasters. They released four influential albums before Dave left to join the band, X, and later embark on a solo career that produced several critically acclaimed albums, including the Grammy Award-winning *Public Domain*. He and Phil reunited in 2014 for their tribute album to Big Bill Broonzy, *Common Ground*, and a blues album, *Lost Time*.

His songs have been recorded by, among others, Los Lobos, Joe Ely, and Little Milton. He has produced recordings for Chris Gaffney, the Derailers, and Tom Russell, and his music has been featured in television shows and movies.

Alvin lives in Los Angeles.

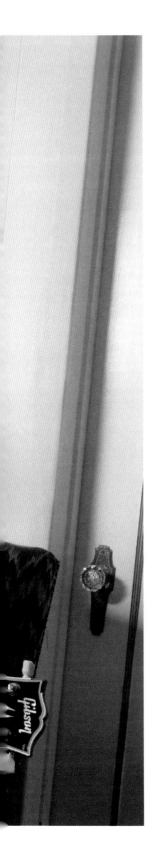

# RAY BENSON

## THE RED 355

I bought a 1961 Gibson 355 with the money I made from my first record deal with United Artists in 1972. I paid Glenn Keener five hundred dollars for it. Glenn was a guitar player, and he did a lot of session work in Nashville. He told me that the guitar used to belong to Leon Rhodes.

Leon was one of my guitar heroes, one of the great guitar players of all time. He played with Ernest Tubb and the Texas Troubadours. He did a lot of session work and was on the Grand Ole Opry for a number of years.

I used that guitar on the road for many years. The 355 is red, and it has a Lone Star beer sticker on it. Once Eric Clapton jammed with us when we were in Atlanta. I have a picture of him playing it.

Some years after I bought the guitar, I sold it to the Hard Rock Café because I needed money. I came to really regret selling it.

Many, many years later, I was talking with a fellow from Gibson. He had worked with the Hard Rock, and I lamented that I had sold that guitar. He told me it was hanging up in the Austin Hard Rock, which was about to close.

I went in to see it and it was hanging in a back corner. You could see it was hurting because nobody was playing it. It was getting hot and dusty.

I decided I wanted to get it back. I offered to trade a Ray Benson model guitar I have. It's a solid body and it's a very nice guitar. They go for a couple thousand bucks.

We worked a deal, and it took a year but, sure enough, it came back. I traded the Ray Benson guitar for it.

Eventually I retired that 355. It just became too valuable, to be honest. It's still a great guitar. I play it occasionally in the studio, and I used it when we had our Asleep at the Wheel fortieth anniversary show. The Ray Benson signature model made by Eastman is modeled after the 355 in a number of ways.

At one point, I asked Leon Rhodes about that guitar and he said, "Ya know Ray, I never owned a Gibson 355."

Philadelphia native RAY BENSON co-founded the western swing band Asleep at the Wheel in 1970. The preeminent band of a genre made famous by Bob Wills and the Texas Playboys, Asleep at the Wheel began in West Virginia. In 1974, Benson moved it to Austin, Texas, at the urging of Willie Nelson.

After more than forty-five years, thirty albums, and ten Grammy awards, Benson remains in front of the band. More than one hundred musicians have filled the ranks of the Wheel during its history.

The singer, songwriter, musician, and producer co-wrote *A Ride With Bob: The Bob Wills Musical* in 2005 to commemorate the hundredth birthday of the Texas legend. In 2011, Benson was named Texan of the Year and was the recipient of the Texas Medal of the Arts Award for Multimedia. He was honored by the Americana Music Association with a Lifetime Achievement Award.

Benson lives in Austin.

# TORONZO CANNON

## THE GIG AND THE JOB

I've always liked Flying V guitars. They have a tone other guitars don't have. The V makes a hollow sound, and I like that. It's not like a 335 or other hollow bodies. My first one was a Gibson, but I sold that to get another Strat.

Then I heard Little Jimmy King's *Live From Monterrey* CD. On the cover, he's playing a white Flying V. There's a slow blues he does on that CD called "Drowning on Dry Land." I listened to that song every day. I needed it like water.

I've had arguments with my friends about bluesmen. They say a bluesman with a straight job don't get the same respect as bluesmen that do it for a living. But I've gotta make the gig and still go to my job. My wife and thirteen-year-old daughter shouldn't have to suffer because I want to be a blues star.

So I sit on the bus all day and I think. I'm a bus driver for the Chicago Transit Authority. If I get an idea for a song, I'll write it down. I don't keep a notebook; I just use memos we get from the CTA. I write about stuff I see around me. I work in a pretty bad neighborhood. I overhear conversations on the bus and sometimes those become ideas for songs.

I remember hearing a woman say, "Girl, it's gettin' on towards Christmas time. I gotta find me a man." I hear a bunch of stuff like that. I like to write songs that people possibly could have lived through.

Years ago, I read an article in a female magazine. This was right after *What's Love Got to Do with It*, the Tina Turner movie, came out. The article said that when a woman is in an abusive relationship, she should always have an extra bank account and keep clothes at a girlfriend's house in case she has to run away. For some reason, that stayed with me, so I wrote a song called, "If You're Woman Enough to Leave Me, I'm Man Enough to See You Go."

> I know about the clothes at your girl friend's house,
> I know about my money in your secret bank account.
> It makes things easier when you plan your getaway,
> Only God and the neighbors know what you do when
>     I'm at work all day.

I play around Chicago, where I have a bit of a name. Three or four times a year I'll go to Europe to play gigs. Joe Moss is another blues guy here in Chicago. Joe was raving about Kurt Wilson guitars, going on about how they were so great to play. I wanted to meet Kurt.

So Joe took me. You can't go to Kurt's on your own. You have to go through somebody. And I can dig it. The guy is working out of his house and he doesn't want a bunch of cats just showing up at his door.

Everything he had to show me was right-handed, and he was feeling bad about that. He wanted to make one for me as a lefty instead of using a righty as a lefty. So I asked him to make a lefty Flying V.

I wanted all Korina because it's a super-light wood. It's like five pounds and it resonates. It resonates better than my Les Pauls.

The neck is modeled after the neck of a '57 Les Paul. The necks on the '58 V are too big. They're too thick and wide. Kurt shaved the neck the way I wanted it. I mean, it's right there. My calluses are hitting the strings right where they should. Then he put my logo on the last fret.

I'm playing the heck out of it, and I've been writing songs for my new CD on that Flying V.

Growing up in his grandfather's house near Theresa's Lounge on Chicago's South Side, **TORONZO CANNON** heard plenty of music.

He didn't buy his first guitar until he was twenty-two. After playing in a reggae band for a couple of years, he was pulled back to the blues. Cannon learned his craft by playing in bands fronted by two of Chicago's finest, Wayne Baker Brooks and Joanna Connor.

After starting his own band in 2001, he recorded three albums for the Delmark label and now records on the Alligator Records label. His most recent album, *The Chicago Way*, was released in 2016. He performs in Chicago and internationally.

By day, he drives a bus for the Chicago Transit Authority, a job he's held much of his adult life. At night, he's a bluesman.

Cannon lives in Chicago.

# ROSANNE CASH

## SOMETHING PERFECT

There are guitars that have always been special to me, but none as special as my signature Martin.

Martin guitars have been connected with my family forever. Dick Boak, who was the director of artist relations at Martin, told me this great story about my dad. When Dick called him about doing a signature guitar, my dad didn't even say hello. He said, "I've been waiting for this phone call all my life."

I felt like that when they called me. It's like the best award in the world to have Martin call and say they want to make a signature model. I don't think someone who is not a guitar player can appreciate the feeling. It's this feeling of legitimacy.

I'm not a great guitar player. I'm a rhythm guitar player, and I didn't need anything fancy. I needed something serviceable, balanced, and beautiful.

My husband John and I designed it. I went crazy with all these ideas, and John was the voice of reason. Also, he had the language to talk about the specs of the guitar, which I didn't. I had an image in my mind, but he had the vocabulary.

I knew three things. I knew I wanted it to be smaller than a dreadnaught because that can overwhelm someone who is five-foot-five. So we chose an orchestra model, which is the OM-28. It's the perfect size for me.

I knew I wanted it to be white. I had been watching clips from 1960s television shows, and I saw Loretta Lynn playing a white electric guitar. I thought that was the coolest thing ever—a white guitar for a woman. But John had to pull me back from that ledge.

He said, "It can't be white white. You have to have real wood." So we got it as white as we could with a very light-colored Adirondack spruce top.

Finally, I knew I wanted the tone to be evenly balanced. That's the problem I've always had with playing guitars. Either the high end sounds great or the low end sounds great. I've never had a really well-balanced guitar sound in concert halls. I wanted an even balance with mid-range sweetness. Not too bright like a bluegrass player or too mellow like a classical guitar. I wanted it right in the middle, and I didn't want them to model it on anything else.

When I first thought about how it would look, I went in a very girly direction. Lots of mother of pearl and lots of stuff on the neck. I wanted my name scrolled on it. John pulled me back from that ledge, too. He said, "It will wear out on you. You've got to get something classic."

It has mother of pearl, but not a lot. And on the headstock, there's a rose. Dick and I looked at pictures of roses for that headstock. There are green leaves on the rose. This is a first for Martin, to have green on a guitar.

After we gave them all the specs, I waited. I was so nervous. I was afraid it was not going to be what I had hoped for. Maybe it would look great but sound terrible or not look good.

When I pulled it out of the case, I strummed it and it had this beautiful resonance. I started crying. It was overwhelming. I have very seldom experienced something perfect, something that exceeded my dreams. I was in tears because this guitar sounded like me and it looked like me. It just fits me so well in every way.

Martin sent me the prototype and number one. I couldn't decide which one sounded better. They are both amazing. I have a daughter who is a guitar player, so at some point, I'll probably give one to her.

Since I've gotten the guitar, I've been on the road. So it's served me in live performance much more than in writing. I find out how it sounds the best when I use it in a performance. I learn how to play certain songs, and it's microscopically different than the way you'd play the same song on another guitar. A guitar has its own personality and the beauty is in trying to find out how it dovetails with the songs you play on it.

I look forward to sitting with it for long periods and writing. There are songs in this guitar, and I'm discovering what those songs are.

Several words describe ROSANNE CASH. Songwriter, singer, musician, and best-selling author come to mind.

Over more than thirty years, she has created a body of work so rich in variety—rock, pop, country, blues, gospel, and Americana—that it's difficult to pigeonhole her style.

Since 1978, she has recorded thirteen albums and won four Grammy Awards. Her 2014 album *The River & the Thread* was awarded three Grammys coming thirty years after her first.

In 2015, she was inducted into the Nashville Songwriters Hall of Fame, joining a long list of prior inductees including Guy Clark, Johnny Cash, Bob Dylan, Willie Nelson, Buddy Holly, and Hank Williams.

She is also the best-selling author of four books including her memoir, *Composed*. Her essays have appeared in the *New York Times*, *Rolling Stone*, and the *Oxford American*.

She lives in New York City with her husband John Leventhal.

# CINDY CASHDOLLAR

## RISEN FROM THE ASHES

I just love old instruments because I think they've lived a life. When I get an old instrument and I open the case, I want to say, "Wow! Where have you been? Where did you come from? What did you do?"

What if you could open up a case and see the history of an instrument? I think there should be a rule: when you own a guitar, there should be a big piece of paper in the case that says, "My name is so-and-so, and I got this guitar and here's what I do." And that piece of paper stays in that case when you pass it along to someone else. It would have an alarm system so that the paper couldn't leave the case.

It's like this little 1940s Gibson lap steel I'm babysitting until it goes on to its owner in Ohio. It's got "Claudine" on the case and "Claudine" written on it. Well, who's Claudine? Who was this cool woman playing this Gibson lap steel in the '40s? I would love to know who she was.

My favorite guitar is a lap steel that my former husband, Frank Campbell, made for me in 1992. It's been everywhere with me. I call it "The Phoenix" because it looks like it's risen from the ashes.

Frank's a musician. He plays bass, he's a recording engineer, and he's a carpenter. He found this old block of maple and, just for fun, he wanted to try and make a lap steel for me. He patterned it after the National New Yorker.

I've used that thing everywhere, with everybody. It's had countless different pickups in it over the years. I like Telecaster pickups so it's always had some kind of Tele pickup in there. It doesn't have a vintage sound, but more of a rock/blues sound to it. I love it.

Frank put up a little tent in the back of his truck so he could spray-paint it because there was no garage where we were living at the time. He used auto paint. It was kind of a dark blue, similar to the old Fender bass color. But it's since gotten darker.

I'll have to refinish it because it's getting hard to see the fret markers. I have to have those, but that's easily fixed. This thing has more dents and dings from the bar being dropped on it. It looks pretty rough. This lap steel sounds amazing, and I'd never part with it. But if I ever did, I'd send it on its way with a piece of paper that says, "It was made with love."

CINDY CASHDOLLAR (yes, a real name) is known for her steel guitar, resonator guitar, and lap steel skills. Originally from Woodstock, she developed her sound playing with Paul Butterfield, Levon Helm, Rick Danko, and bluegrass stylists John Herald and Bill Keith.

She moved to Austin after Ray Benson hired her to play steel guitar with Asleep at the Wheel. She earned five Grammy Awards for her work with the band.

She has toured and recorded with Van Morrison, Dave Alvin, Jorma Kaukonen, Redd Volkaert, and others. Her work can be heard on Bob Dylan's Grammy-winning *Time Out of Mind*. The first female inducted into the Texas Steel Guitar Hall of Fame, she was also named to the Texas Music Hall of Fame. She has been a frequent guest on *A Prairie Home Companion*. Her debut CD, *Slide Show*, features both slide and steel guitar.

She lives in Woodstock, New York.

# GUY CLARK

## A CHUNK OF WOOD

I was sixteen or seventeen when I started playing the guitar. I was living in a little town called Rockport, down on the Gulf Coast, which is where I went to junior high and high school. I just had cheap Mexican border guitars. The first one I got, I took apart to fix because it didn't play right.

Working with wood is something that's always come naturally to me from the time I was a kid. I was born in Monahans, Texas. In West Texas, one of the first things you get is a pocketknife and a whetstone. You make your own toys. I've always been partial to working with wood. From the very beginning, I've worked on friends' guitars, repaired guitars, and built guitars.

I did some guitar building in two different spurts. I built some in Texas—some classical guitars—and probably a few of them survived. I don't own one, but I know where maybe one or two of them are. They are probably not very good guitars. They looked okay, but there are some elements that I just didn't know about at the time.

I started building again about ten years ago. I have almost all of those guitars. I gave three or four away, but I still have the first one. It's a flamenco guitar. I had been carrying the wood around for twenty or thirty years.

The flamenco guitar is a nylon-string guitar. It originated in Spain in the 1850s. It was originally a percussion instrument and was made to accompany dancers and singers. It wasn't until much later that it became a solo instrument.

I'm not really a flamenco player. It's the first style of guitar that I became interested in that I learned to play. Fairly soon I moved to a steel string guitar. But I have always loved flamenco guitars. It's a fascinating method of construction, a nineteenth-century technology. Everything is done with hand tools—no power tools necessary. You can start with a chunk of wood and end up with a guitar. I've found that really satisfying.

I play one on stage and I use them exclusively when I'm writing. There are two or three that are very good guitars. I use them all the time. Guitars should be tools. They're meant to be played.

Arguably, one of them is the best guitar I've ever played. It has all the volume you want. The tone quality is quite good. It's just a great guitar.

GUY CLARK (1941–2016) was already forging a reputation as a songwriter by the time he released his first album, *Old No. 1*, in 1975, due in part to Jerry Jeff Walker's cover of Clark's "L.A. Freeway." Over the next forty years, Clark became a highly respected and honored songwriter and recording artist in both country and folk music. His last album, *My Favorite Picture of You*, won the Grammy for Best Folk Album in 2013.

Dozens of musicians—including Ricky Skaggs, Vince Gill, and Asleep at the Wheel—have made the charts with Clark-penned songs. His own critically acclaimed albums included *Texas Cookin'* and *Boats to Build*. His 1983 *Better Days* included one of his best-known songs, "Randall Knife," a reflection about his father. *This One's for Him: A Tribute to Guy Clark*, featuring thirty-three artists, won the Americana Album of the Year in 2012.

# JOANNA CONNOR

## THE GREAT MISTAKE

I was touring Europe and I had some issues with my guitar, so I took it to a Gibson-authorized repairman in Germany. He looked at it and said the guitar was kind of a mistake.

I said, "What do you mean?"

"The radius on the neck is not up to specs," he said. "But whoever did this, this guitar is tremendous."

I'm not a technical person, but he said the way the neck was made was a little bit different from most of the models from that year. Even though they're made on a machine to a degree, I guess this one somehow came out different. He played it and said, "Man, this guitar is amazing." I got the great mistake.

The guitar was part of an endorsement deal with Gibson. I had moved to Chicago a few years earlier. I was only twenty-two, and everyone thought I was crazy. I was incredibly fearless back then. I think a lot of people dream of things, but don't actually go and do it. You have to take that step.

I had a pretty good handle on the blues, but I wanted to go to the city where it was played every day. I wanted to learn. When I saw Dion Payton, his approach to rhythm guitar and singing just blew me away. I followed Dion all the time and I picked his brain.

Dion turned out to be incredibly tough. He was like the football coach of music. He'd yell. He'd swear. He showed no mercy. One of the reasons I started playing slide in regular tuning is because he wouldn't allow me time to pick up another guitar or put it in open tuning. If you're going to play slide, you've just got do it and do it smoothly. Play your solo and get back to rhythm. To this day, I pride myself on that.

I was always good at rhythm guitar. I could fingerpick and play slide and I played a little lead, but Dion was a perfectionist. He taught me to make every note count. Even if there's a million notes, you play them cleanly. Have good rhythm chops. He taught me to listen to the band and fit in the groove.

Within four months of moving to Chicago, I got a gig playing with the 43rd Street Blues Band, which was the house band at the Checkerboard Lounge. It was a huge learning experience. I had to prove I had something going on. As a young white girl, I was a novelty. One of Buddy Guy's sons plays guitar. He said his dad told him, "Yeah, that girl really couldn't play shit back then, but she's great now." And he was right.

In 1989, I went to the NAMM Show in Chicago. I had recorded my first CD for Blind Pig the year before. It was called *Believe It!* I dropped off my press kit with my CD with different manufacturers at the show. Gibson called me to offer an endorsement deal. I was blown away. Part of the deal was they gave me a guitar. I went to New York where Gibson had a showroom just off Times Square. I knew I wanted a Les Paul and I picked out a Goldtop. I liked the way it felt in my hands.

About six weeks later, I got a guitar in the mail. It was the 1960 Les Paul Classic Reissue, not the Goldtop I had ordered. I wrestled with the idea of calling Gibson and telling them I'd rather have a Goldtop, but I decided I didn't want to wait another six weeks, so I kept the sunburst. I'm really glad I did. This guitar is awesome.

I had a few other guitars. I had three other Gibsons and a Strat, but I had to sell them when I was pregnant with my daughter because I wasn't playing for like a month. I have two kids and I've always put them first financially. Mom buying another guitar wasn't ever on the list. All I have is one acoustic and one electric guitar and it's the 1960 Les Paul Classic Reissue.

I would like to have a few more instruments, but right now, this is working for me. I use the 1960 Reissue, my acoustic, and I go to work.

The thing about having only one guitar for a long time is that I feel like I know the instrument beneath my fingers so well. I like playing other guitars, but I know that one. I know what it does. It's like a part of me. It's my baby. Even if I had other guitars, I wonder if I would play them.

JOANNA CONNOR made her way to Chicago in 1985 from Worcester, Massachusetts, to hone her blues skills and learn from the best. She landed a spot in the 43rd Street Blues Band a few months after her arrival, playing behind up-and-coming artists as well as some legendary figures in blues and soul music.

Connor has released ten albums beginning with *Believe It!*, her 1989 release on the Blind Pig Records label. Extensive touring brought her to the attention of blues fans in the United States, Canada, and Europe. She continues to play and tour and can be seen with her band at Kingston Mines and other clubs in the Chicago area.

She lives in Chicago.

# PETER COOPER

One of my main influences and a guy I've tried to steal from at every turn is Tom T. Hall.

I think he recognized the extent to which I was trying to steal from him. And he decided he would be okay with that. He decided he would be honored rather than ticked off. He has always supported my music.

In early 2010, I saw him at a music function. He said, "Hey, when can you come by the house?"

"Anytime," I said.

He said, "Come sooner than later. I've got something for you."

I went to his house and on the floor was a baby blue Martin case from the 1970s. It was open and inside was a black Ovation guitar with the "TTH" symbol for Tom T. Hall engraved on the front. A typed letter rested on top of the guitar. That letter is now framed in my house.

It's dated February 27, 2010. It says: "I'm making you a gift of my Ovation guitar, number 237928, black, with my TTH logo on the front in gold."

The rest of the letter goes on to tell the history of the guitar. It was his onstage guitar . . . his touring guitar . . . the one he played every night.

He always took his songwriting guitar, a little Martin, on the road with him. But when he was touring Australia, he wanted to take as little as possible, so he just took the Ovation. He said normally the Ovation was like a tuxedo. He didn't want to see it until he was ready to go onstage.

Though he didn't have his songwriting guitar for this Australia trip, he did have some songwriting ideas. So he went to his hotel room and wrote two songs on the Ovation. One was "Bill Monroe for Breakfast" and the other was "Little Bitty."

The letter goes on to say that, when he got home, he emptied the contents of his briefcase into his desk drawer before going to Atlanta to attend a party with his life-long friend, Johnny Cash. It was the wrap party for Cash's movie, *Murder in Coweta County*.

Tom T. said in the letter, "At the party, John and I sang a few songs for the cast and crew. After the party, John asked me for something to put in his museum. I handed him this Ovation guitar." So for several years the guitar languished in the museum at The House of Cash and the songs languished in the drawer.

Then the letter talks about when Tom T. was looking for songs to demo with some friends who had a recording set-up. He went through his desk drawer and found his notes from the Australian tour. "Little Bitty" was not quite finished. He read through the lyrics, wrote a last verse, and then did a demo. His publisher, Tom Collins, played the song for Alan Jackson. He recorded it, and it became a number one country song.

Tom T. recorded the other song he found in the drawer for his *Home Grown* album. "Bill Monroe for Breakfast" became a number one bluegrass song.

In 2010, Johnny Cash's son called Tom T. By that time, Johnny had died and they had closed The House of Cash museum. John Carter Cash said, "I've got one of your guitars and I want to give it back."

The letter ends, "Now you have it. All the best, Tom T. Hall."

When he gave the Ovation to me, he said, "So, only two songs have been written on this guitar and they were both number ones. Good luck, son."

I've written one song on it called "Opening Day." It's about the first day of the baseball season, when everybody is tied for first place. It's a song about hope and optimism and how all that soon fades.

Tom T. said he gave Cash the guitar off his back. I don't think he gave it to him with a case, but if he did, it would have been an Ovation case. But he gave it to me in a beautiful Martin hard-shell case. Johnny Cash and June Carter Cash often played Martins. So who knows whose hands have held this case? That's the mystery element to this guitar.

The Ovation is my most treasured guitar. I've played it on the radio and in the studio. I play it all the time around the house. Sometimes it's my lullaby guitar for my young son.

I don't think Tom T. gives away guitars willy-nilly. So I believe there's a kind of trust inherent in this gift, that he gave it to me for a reason. The only two songs he wrote on it were number ones that spoke to a lot of people. That's inspiring because you're holding something special, and you want to bring something special to it.

I think he knew I would care for it and care about it and that he thought I would be the right owner for it. I draw inspiration from that. If I'm working on that guitar and writing a song, I'm not going to let the weak line hang around.

I like guitars with a story behind them. In this case, I got a guitar with a story behind it from The Storyteller himself.

PETER COOPER wears many hats—singer, songwriter, musician, performer, college professor, and writer.

With his songwriting partner Eric Brace, Cooper produced *I Love: Tom T. Hall's Songs of Fox Hollow*, which received a Grammy nomination for Best Children's Album in 2012. Cooper and Brace have three albums to their credit, the most recent, *Eric Brace & Peter Cooper: The Comeback Album*, released in 2013. His solo work includes *Depot Light: Songs of Eric Taylor*, and his session work includes recordings with Todd Snider, Emmylou Harris, and Ricky Skaggs.

Once a music columnist for the *Tennessean*, Cooper now works at the Country Music Hall of Fame as a writer and editor.

He lives in Nashville.

# DAN DUGMORE

## BLACKA AND THE BANDIT

When I joined Linda Ronstadt's band in October 1974, I had a 1968 Goldtop Les Paul. In those days, you only had one guitar. Nowadays, everybody has a whole slew of them. But back then, if you needed another guitar, you usually had to sell one to buy some other kind.

On my first tour with Linda, we were playing a two-night gig in Cleveland. The roadie brought the guitars up to the dressing room and went back to get more. When he was coming back up the stairs, he saw a guy going out the second-story window with my gold Les Paul. It was gone.

We called the promoter in the next town and asked him to contact guitar dealers and have them bring any Les Paul Goldtops they might have for me to try. Linda said, "When you find one you like, we'll buy it for you."

I kept trying Goldtops at all these gigs, and I couldn't find one I liked.

About two weeks later, we were in Hartford, Connecticut. A dealer there told me, "I don't have any Les Paul Goldtops. You'll have to use this black one." It was a 1968 model like the gold one. That was the year Gibson started reissuing Les Pauls.

I plugged it in at the sound check and the whole band looked over at me. We decided it had the best sound. I said, "I want this guitar."

Linda bought that one for me and that's been my main guitar since that night in 1974. I've used it on so many recordings over the years. We nicknamed her "Blacka."

I've played a lot of Les Pauls, but this one seems to have a voice of its own. I can't really say what it is, but it's a very pleasing tone. You know, Neil Young played that black Les Paul. Blacka is kind of like a Neil Young-sounding guitar.

Most people want me to break out Blacka when they ask me to play. I played her for the solo on Linda Ronstadt's "Lose Again." I also played her on James Taylor's "Everyday" and Martina McBride's "My Baby Loves Me the Way I Am."

A couple of years after the Goldtop was stolen, I got a telegram from the Cleveland police department telling me they'd recovered it. The guy had pawned it for seventy-five dollars and he didn't go back to get it.

Back in those days, those guitars were worth about five hundred dollars, so that's what my insurance coverage was for. Linda had bought me the black one, so I had collected the five hundred dollars from my insurance agent. I was ahead in the game.

I asked my insurance agent, "What do I do? Should I send you back a check for five hundred dollars?" He said, "No, we legally own the guitar. But you don't know what's happened to it. You might not want it. Let me get it."

When it was stolen, it already had a broken headstock and gouges all over it. When my insurance agent opened up the case, he said, "Oh my God, it's really beaten up!"

I didn't tell him that I was the one who beat it up.

He said, "What do you think it's worth? A couple of hundred bucks?"

I said, "That would be great."

I made out like a bandit.

A native of California, DAN DUGMORE is a veteran of the country rock music that dominated the radio airwaves in the 1970s and 1980s. Best known for his work on the pedal steel guitar, he is a multi-instrumentalist.

His recording and tour credits span four decades. His work can be heard on recordings by, among others, Linda Rondstadt, James Taylor, ZZ Top, Kid Rock, Dave Stewart, Tim McGraw, Faith Hill, Martina McBride, David Crosby, Warren Zevon, Keith Urban, and Willie Nelson. Dugmore toured with Linda Ronstadt's band for fourteen years, followed by eleven years with James Taylor.

A studio musician, he has played on some seventeen hundred albums and has been named Steel Guitar Player of the Year four times by the Academy of Country Music.

Dugmore lives in Nashville.

# TOMMY EMMANUEL

## THE MOUSE

"The mouse" is the nickname I gave this guitar. The mouse that roared. It's a little guitar, but it has a massive sound.

The guitars I use are made by Maton Guitars in Melbourne, Australia. I picked up my first one in 1960. In 1992, they rang me and said, "We think we've made something special. We want you to come check it out." So I went to the factory to try this guitar. The body size is like an orchestra model, and it's made of indigenous Australian wood. The back and sides are Queensland maple, with a spruce top and rosewood fingerboard. It has a natural-sounding pickup.

I plugged it in and it sounded amazing. I said, "I'm not leaving here without this guitar."

They said, "But we're not finished with it yet."

"Yes, you are. I'm buying it."

I fell in love with the instrument, and I used it on everything. After spending some time on the road with it, though, I told Maton, "You're right. You need to make the electronics lighter." And they did. The tone of the guitar has just gotten deeper and bigger.

I was on a world tour, playing a show in Amsterdam at a club called The Panama. The place was packed, and they were a wild audience.

I finished the show and was going to the merchandise table to sign autographs for people who bought CDs. I put my guitar in the case and left it on the side of the stage. I didn't make it to the table. The crowd rushed me. I was cornered, so I just started signing autographs.

I happened to look over the top of the crowd at the stage, and I saw people who were not part of the crew up there. I said to the guy who played before me to keep an eye on the gear.

When I finished signing autographs, I went backstage and packed up the rest of my gear. "Where's the mouse?" I asked. We looked and looked, but it was gone.

We went to the police and they told me I may as well say goodbye to it because I was never going to see it again.

The next morning, we went searching for pawnshops. We discovered there aren't any in Amsterdam. There were people setting up stands to sell things in the streets, and I asked a guy where somebody would unload a stolen item. He said, "We don't steal things around here." He was offended by the question. I told him my guitar had been stolen the night before, and I was looking for it. Where might somebody unload it? He said again, "We don't steal things around here." That's all he would say to me.

Later at lunch, a waiter came over and asked, "Are you Mr. Emmanuel?" When I said yes, he said, "I have a message for you. Somebody found your guitar. It's in an Irish pub in the red light district."

We ran out of the restaurant and jumped in a car. When we got to the pub, the girl behind the bar said, "Don't worry, I've got it." She introduced herself as Linda, and she put the guitar on the bar.

Apparently, one guy who was rather enthusiastic about the show had been standing at the front of the stage. He saw me leave the guitar and he took it. He went to a party afterward at Linda's apartment. He was a bit inebriated, and he ended up going to sleep on the floor. He left the guitar sitting in the corner.

Linda was getting ready for work that morning, and she saw the guitar. She looked in the case and knew it was my guitar because she was also at the show. She found a business card from my British agent. Phone calls went around the world. My agent called my manager, who had just arrived in Australia. She found my merchandise guy in Amsterdam, who found me at the restaurant.

If Linda hadn't noticed it, that guy might have gotten up, taken the guitar home, and I'd never have seen it again.

I still have the mouse and have used it on countless recordings, including my most popular acoustic recording, "Only."

Born in Australia, **TOMMY EMMANUEL** got his first guitar at four. By six, he was playing in a family band, organized by his father. Inspired by Chet Atkins, Emmanuel became known for his finger-style guitar technique.

He played drums for Goldrush, a band that included his brother, and later played guitar for the Southern Star Band and Dragon. In demand for studio work, he began to release his own records, beginning with *From Out of Nowhere* (1979). He has recorded more than two dozen solo albums, including *It's Never Too Late* (2015).

In 1997, he teamed with Atkins for *The Day Finger Pickers Took Over the World*. The record, Atkins's last, included "Smokey Mountain Lullaby," which was nominated for a Grammy for Country Instrumental Performance. Emmanuel was nominated in the same category in 2007 for "Gameshow Rag/Cannonball Rag," from *The Mystery*.

Emmanuel lives in Nashville.

# ALEJANDRO ESCOVEDO

## THOUSANDS OF SONGS

What I love about guitars is that they're the coolest instrument. Guitars represent rock 'n' roll to me.

I don't think of myself as a guitar player. I'm a songwriter, and I use the guitar as a tool to write songs. It's the only instrument I can play, and I play it very marginally. I was twenty-four when I started, and, I have to tell you, it took me a long time to learn to play.

I wanted to be a filmmaker. That's what I wanted to do in life. The only way I got into a band was by making a movie about the worst band in the world. Since we couldn't play, we were that band.

Thank God, punk rock came at that time because it swallowed us up and gave us some sort of validity. That was in '75 or '76. It's taken a long time, but I feel okay on guitar now.

In about 1981 or 1982, I came through Kansas City with the band Rank and File. It was then I met two guys, Matt Kesler and Jim Strahm. Later, when I was in the True Believers, we started to play with the band Absolute Ceiling from Kansas City. Jim and some other guys were in that band. Eventually, Jim and Matt had a store called Midwestern Musical Exchange in Kansas City. They became my best friends.

Jim was a collector of all things Americana. Everything from Airstreams to clothes to cowboy boots to leather jackets to Harleys. And guitars. He had a beautiful collection of guitars.

At one point, I was playing guitars that other people had given me. They were all different. Some worked and some didn't. I was

trying out all kinds of things. Jim came to me one day and said, "You need this guitar. This is a guitar that you should have." They gave me Matt's 1956 Gibson J-50.

That acoustic guitar changed my life. I wrote more songs on it than on any guitar I've ever had. Someone told me once about this old man who walked in a music store and started talking about guitars. He was asked why new guitars don't sound as good as old ones. He said it was because they don't have any songs in them yet.

That J-50 has thousands of songs in it. You feel it. You can hear it. You can just look at it and know it's been places. I don't write on any guitar but this one.

Jim passed away from cancer a few years ago, and it was a big blow to all of us who loved him. He was a close friend. He went on tour with me. We shared deep, deep secrets with each other.

The guitar represents not only our friendship but also all the tunes I've written and how I learned to write songs, how I learned to compose songs, and how I learned to arrange songs. It all came through that guitar.

Everyone who has ever picked it up just can't put it down. I've recorded a lot with it in the studio. I've got a Highlander pickup in it and it's got that classic Stones/Keith Richards thing going. It sounds like an old instrument, but it's got a clarity and a beautiful tone, a very wooden, organic sound.

That guitar is almost like a security blanket. I go to it when I'm not feeling well. I'll pick it up and just start strumming. I'll sing songs with it and it really brings me to a place that is calm, peaceful.

It's just always been stellar.

A native of San Antonio, Texas, ALEJANDRO ESCOVEDO has had a long and varied career. After moving to California, the singer-songwriter performed with the Nuns, a punk rock group, in the 1970s. He returned to Texas, where he played with the influential band Rank and File. He then joined his brother, Javier, in the True Believers, establishing himself as a force in Americana and alt country music. The band toured heavily, often opening for Los Lobos.

Escovedo's first solo effort was the 1992 release *Gravity*, followed by, among others, *A Man Under the Influence* (2001), *Street Songs of Love* (2010), and *Big Station* (2012). *Por Vida: A Tribute to the Songs of Alejandro Escovedo* was released in 2004 as part of an outpouring of support from fellow musicians following his illness from Hepatitis C. Fully recovered, Escovedo continues to write, record, and perform.

He lives in Dallas.

# DENNY FREEMAN

## ONE NIGHT AT THE CONTINENTAL

I've never had more than a few guitars, and I've mainly played Stratocasters. I've always been a Fender guy, a Strat guy. Usually, no matter what else I had, I had a Strat.

But a few years ago, I decided I wanted a Flying V and a Gibson Firebird. I guess I'd told Charlie Sexton about wanting a V. I first met Charlie in the early '80s. His mom would bring him and his brother, Will, along to hear bands she liked. She'd take them to see the Fabulous Thunderbirds, a band I was in called the Cobras, and a few other bands.

Charlie had already started playing by then. He was twelve and Will was ten. Charlie, he'd wear sport coats and grease his hair back. He'd play guitar, and Will would play bass. When their mom brought them to gigs, they would both sit in. And they could *play*. Before the night was over, you'd look over and see Will asleep on one of the tables.

In 1999, Charlie got the gig playing guitar with Bob Dylan's band. He left that in 2002. A couple of years after Charlie quit Bob's band, I joined. I played with Bob from 2005 until August 2009. Then when I left, Charlie rejoined the band.

About a year after I left Dylan's band, I was at the Continental Club in Austin, playing a gig with Bill Carter and the Blame. The band included Bill, Andy Salmon, Chris Layton, Charlie, and me. Bill had a rotating cast of characters for the band, but the main band had Charlie and me on guitar and Andy on bass. Drummers

came and went, but Chris was usually the drummer at the time. We didn't play every week, or even every month, because we were all doing different stuff. But when everybody was available, Bill would pull us together to play.

Charlie was in Dylan's band at the time, and they were in Austin for a show. They had the night off, so Charlie was there to play with Bill's band.

We were hanging out before the gig in the back room at the Continental. Some of the guys from Dylan's band were there. So was Bob's manager. Charlie walked in with a guitar case and handed it to me. Then they all sang "Happy Birthday." I opened it up and there was a Gibson Flying V. It really kind of freaked me out.

The birthday card was signed by Bill Carter, Charlie, Chris Layton, Andy Salmon, and Connie Vaughan.

I had forgotten that I'd told Charlie I wanted a Flying V. He'd picked one out at Austin Vintage Guitars. When he went back a few days later to get it, it was gone. So he bought a different one. He thought this was a better one anyway.

Almost every time I play, I say, "What am I gonna play?" If I'm gonna play with Bill, I'll use that guitar. Same with Charlie. If I'm gonna do something with him, I'll take it.

The V is cool and I really like the way it looks. It was really sweet of them to give it to me.

Although primarily a blues guitar player, DENNY FREEMAN has also played piano and organ as a solo artist and with other musicians on the road and in the studio. The Texas-born Freeman has toured and recorded with a wide variety of artists, including Stevie Ray Vaughan, Jimmie Vaughan, and Taj Mahal.

In 1970, he moved to Austin, Texas. He was a member of the house band at the famous Antone's, playing guitar and piano behind such legends as Otis Rush, Albert Collins, Buddy Guy, and Jimmy Rogers.

Freeman was part of Bob Dylan's band from 2005 to 2009, and he plays on Dylan's 2006 Grammy-winning album, *Modern Times*. He has recorded five mainly instrumental albums, including *Out of the Blue* (1987), *Twang Bang* (2006), and his most recent, *Diggin' on Dylan*, a collection of sixteen Dylan songs.

Freeman lives in Austin.

# BILL FRISELL

## OLD WOOD

Robert Quine was a friend of mine. He was a guitar player who played with Lou Reed and Richard Hell and the Voidoids. He did a lot in the punk world. We played on a couple of recordings together. One was a Charles Mingus tribute album. We also played on a Marianne Faithfull record in the '80s.

Quine was a fanatic guitar collector. He bought hundreds of guitars. He'd hang out in all the guitar stores and just wander around. Almost every day, Quine would go to Carmine Street Guitars in New York. He became close with the owner, Rick Kelly.

Without going into too much detail, some years ago, Quine had some hard times. His wife had passed away and he had some problems. He ended up committing suicide. When some time had passed and he wasn't coming into the store, Rick became concerned and called the police. That's how they found out what happened.

Around this time, I was in LA with another friend, Marc Ribot. Great guitar player. We were working on the soundtrack to *Walk the Line*, the Johnny Cash movie. Marc said Rick Kelly had all of Bob Quine's guitars and was selling them. I thought I should check that out.

I went to Rick's store. I said, "I'm Bill and I'm a friend of Bob Quine." He immediately knew who I was. He had listened to some of my recordings. We started talking, reminiscing about Quine. I noticed on the wall was one of the guitars I played the last time I was at Quine's apartment. It was a blue Telecaster. I just had to have it, so I bought it. That was my introduction to Rick.

Rick said, "Come in the back and I'll show you these guitars I'm making." He's got a little shop. There's sawdust everywhere. He just loves these guitars and loves making them. Clearly, he's not doing this for the money. I think he loves having people play them.

What's really inspiring is that Rick builds from scratch. He's not buying pre-made necks and bodies. He cuts them out, sands them, and shapes them. He does everything himself. It's really the old school way of doing it.

He'd gotten a pine beam from a loft in the Bowery where Jim Jarmusch, the film director, lived. The ends had rotted so they had to take these gigantic pieces of wood out to renovate the place. These beams were two hundred years old.

The problem with a lot of new guitars is the wood is so new and it's still wet. Rick got me intrigued with the idea of having a guitar made from really old, dried-out wood. I also liked that he got that wood from Jim Jarmusch's loft. I just love his movies. I'm a big fan.

Rick's guitars are modeled after the first Telecasters. There's nothing wrong with putting a Telecaster-type guitar together using pre-made parts. You can make great stuff that way. I don't have anything against them. I've got plenty of those. But this was like getting a new guitar with super-old wood.

The neck is made from some strange wood called padauk. I'd never heard of it, but it looks like rosewood. He doesn't put a heavy finish on it, so the wood is allowed to breathe and vibrate. It's a thin white coating, and you can see a lot of the wood grain. It's very similar to early Fender finishes. But it's a guitar made from wood from Jim Jarmusch's loft in New York.

One evening, my daughter and my wife and I were talking about New York. I said maybe someday I'll get to play on a Jim Jarmusch soundtrack, and I'll make enough money to get an apartment in New York. That same night, I turned on the TV and there's a Jim Jarmusch movie on called *The Limits of Control*. I watched it almost to the end before I realized it was me on the soundtrack.

I once played on an album by a band called Earth. Somehow this album turned up as one of the main things on the soundtrack. So in this roundabout way, I did end up being on a Jim Jarmusch soundtrack.

I wrote to Rick Kelly and I told him the whole story. About Bob Quine being my friend who passed away. Which led me to Rick's store. That led me to him building this guitar made from a piece of Jim Jarmusch's apartment, and somehow I end up playing on a Jim Jarmusch soundtrack.

Rick wrote back and said Jim had invited him to the premiere of *The Limits of Control* and told him to pay particular attention to a certain scene. In the movie, one of the characters carries around a violin case. There's this scene where he talks about the wood in the violin. He explains how molecules react differently when the wood is old, and how that makes for a better instrument. Jarmusch had used word for word what Rick had told him about his philosophy about the old wood used in guitars

In this weird, convoluted way, both Rick Kelly and I ended up in this Jim Jarmusch movie. I just love how all of this stuff is connected.

The discography of **BILL FRISELL** is lengthy, but the titles alone do not convey the depth and breadth of work by a guitarist revered by his peers and in demand by other artists. His work ranges from pop and rock to bluegrass, blues and roots, as well as jazz. His technique erases the boundaries associated with those genres.

A seasoned, Grammy-winning artist, the Denver native has collaborated with a diverse array of artists, including Ron Carter, Paul Simon, Lucinda Williams, McCoy Tyner, and David Sanborn.

With more than thirty albums to his credit, Frisell has also worked on numerous film soundtracks, including *Walk the Line*, the Academy Award-winning movie about the life of Johnny Cash.

Bill Frisell lives in Seattle.

# ELIZA GILKYSON

## THE GOYA AND THE GIBSON

My first guitar was a Mexican-made, nylon-string acoustic. It was 1963 and I was thirteen. It seems like a lot of kids start playing on nylon-string guitars and then change to steel later. Steel strings are tough to start on if you don't have calluses on your fingers.

We actually drove from LA to Tijuana, Mexico, accompanied by my guitar teacher, Carson Parks, and his little brother, Van Dyke Parks, both of whom at the time played in our dad's band, the Easy Riders. There were some good Mexican luthiers making decent guitars if you knew what to look for. We walked around Tijuana and picked out several guitars after playing them.

A year later, I went to Wallach's Music City on Sunset and Vine in Hollywood with my dad, the songwriter Terry Gilkyson. Back then, there were very few music stores and Wallach's was the big one. It was a big deal to go there. The store had the names of all their client artists written high on the wall of the sales room, and "Terry Gilkyson" was up there.

Dad let me pick out whatever guitar I wanted for my birthday. They brought out a bunch of different guitars and I played them. I chose a Goya. It was a special thrill to have my "famous" dad buy me my guitar. It was a memorable day for me because I felt my dad was openly recognizing that I was choosing the music path. I think this was his way of welcoming me into that world.

I later gave the Goya to my brother, Tony. I moved it on because I wanted a steel-string guitar. Tony also moved it on because he wasn't playing it. I think he may have sold it for fifty bucks.

When I was young, I just didn't have an emotional attachment to any guitar, and that's also how I lost my dad's 1948 Gibson. It was an L1 or an L2, and he had given it to me. I later traded it in for almost nothing toward a Martin. Years later, I thought, my God, this was my dad's guitar. It was a beautiful, old Gibson, and I let it go. But I did that a lot with guitars in those days.

In 1992, I was touring with Andreas Vollenweider. We were playing at the convention center in Miami. I got word that someone wanted to come backstage and bring me a gift. I didn't know the person so I rather reluctantly agreed to let him come backstage.

Here comes this guy I don't recognize carrying a beat-up guitar case. He opened it up, pulled out this old, pretty guitar and asked, "Do you recognize this?" I told him no, I didn't.

He said he got it from Tony years ago, but I thought he had his story wrong. It had darkened so much, I didn't recognize it. It was very blond when I owned it, but over the years, it had aged to a beautiful rich, warm patina. Finally, I noticed the Goya name on the headstock.

I was flabbergasted.

To have it come back was very touching. There are a million ways he could have gone with that. He could have saved it for his own kid. But to bring it to me . . . that was quite a righteous thing to do.

My dad was still alive then, so it wasn't as meaningful as it is now. Since I had lost that Gibson, it meant a lot more to me to have the Goya, which I still use for recording today.

ELIZA GILKYSON is a singer-songwriter and guitarist with more than twenty solo recordings to her credit, including *Land of Milk and Honey* (2004) and *The Nocturne Diaries* (2014), both nominated for Grammy Awards.

Her songs have been recorded by such artists as Joan Baez, Rosanne Cash, and Tom Rush. She has toured extensively as a solo artist and in support of Richard Thompson, Patty Griffin, and Mary Chapin Carpenter, among others.

In 2010, she teamed with John Gorka and Lucy Kaplansky to form Red Horse. Their debut album topped the folk music charts. In 2014, Gilkyson recorded "Before the Deluge" for *Looking into You: A Tribute to Jackson Browne*.

A member of the Austin Music Hall of Fame, she has won many Folk Alliance and Austin Music Awards, including the 2014 Songwriter of the Year. Gilkyson co-founded 5604 Manor, a resource center that promotes political activism and community involvement.

She lives in Austin.

# JOHN HAMMOND

In 1992, I was playing a show in Kendal, which is in the Lake District of England. A guy came backstage between sets and showed me a guitar he had just made. His name was Vinnie Smith, and he worked with a guy named David Stubbs. Stubbs's name is inside the guitar, but it was made by Smith. He couldn't put his name on it because he was on welfare at the time. I think he was trying to hide the income.

I had a nice guitar, but it didn't compare to this one. It has koa wood on the back and sides with a cedar top. I've had a Martin M-18 for forty years. It's like a triple O size. I'm most comfortable with that shape. This guitar has a triple O shape, too, but the body is much deeper.

It was just incredible. It was also for sale.

I asked him how much. It was twenty-five hundred pounds, which at the time was nearly five thousand dollars. That was a little out of my league, so I pretty much wrote it off.

When I explained I couldn't afford it, he said, "Can you write me a letter saying you played it and you like it?" I said I would. I tried in the letter to describe the great balance and depth it had, but it was very hard.

I thought I'd never see that guitar again. But about a month later, when I was at home, I got a call from my agent. He said, "Do you know a guy in England named Vinnie Smith?"

I didn't remember the name, but my wife overheard the conversation and said, "That's the guy who showed you that guitar."

My agent said, "He wants you to have the guitar and he'll sell it to you for cost."

"How much is cost?"

He said five hundred dollars.

I was going back to England later that year on a tour with John Lee Hooker, so I arranged for Vinnie to come to the concert with the guitar.

Sure enough, he came to the show, he gave me the guitar, and I gave him the money. He also had a Calton case made for it. The case cost more than the guitar.

I've got all these other guitars in a closet, but this is the one I take to all my gigs. It's the one I feel most at ease playing on stage, at home, everywhere.

There are twelve guitars with David Stubbs's name in them, and that's it. He is no longer in business. Mine is number seven.

It was spotless when I got it. It is not spotless now. It's been through all the bars and clubs I've worked in. There's airplane travel, trains, and buses, whatever. It's been knocked around, but it sounds better than ever.

I've owned many guitars in fifty-four years of playing. But this is the one I've enjoyed most. It's my favorite. It's the kind of guitar that makes you want to play and sing.

JOHN HAMMOND is one of music's most accomplished acoustic blues artists with a career that spans six decades. Hammond's self-titled debut on Vanguard Records in 1962 was the first of more than thirty albums, including his most recent effort, the 2014 *Timeless*.

Hammond, who has played more than four thousand shows, has been nominated for numerous Grammy Awards, winning in 1985 for *Blues Explosion*, a compilation from the Montreux Jazz Festival.

He has performed or recorded with dozens of artists, including Jimi Hendrix, Eric Clapton, Muddy Waters, and Howlin' Wolf. Hammond was the Blues Music Award winner for Acoustic Artist of the Year in 2011, the same year he was inducted into the Blues Hall of Fame. In 2012, he was inducted into the New York Blues Hall of Fame.

Hammond wrote the soundtrack for the 1970 Dustin Hoffman film, *Little Big Man*.

He lives in New Jersey.

# DAVID HOLT

## SARA JANE'S TUNE

In 1989, my wife was driving our daughter to school on a rainy day when the car hydroplaned and crashed into a pickup truck.

They were both in intensive care for seven days. My ten-year-old daughter, Sara Jane, died. My wife survived.

It took me twelve years to get back on my feet. I was performing the whole time, and I continued to do all the things I had to do. I had been playing mountain music professionally since 1973 and was well known as a banjo player. I was on TV, and I played lots of concerts. I had a good career.

But my whole world was turned upside down. Playing mountain music and continuing to perform was healing for me. The banjo was really helpful because it's a positive instrument . . . an instrument of joy. But there was no music that I had in me that could reach down in my soul and bring the pain to the surface and express it.

I got to a point where I didn't know if I wanted to be alive any longer. I felt like I couldn't handle it. My heart was broken. I couldn't even come close to expressing that pain musically.

I was at my lowest point about two years after Sara Jane died. It was then that I got this guitar.

My mother's plumber just happened to have a resophonic guitar. He didn't want it. He knew that I played music, so he gave it to me. The name on the guitar is "Airline." It was made in the '60s by Valco and sold through Montgomery Ward. It's got a regular style O resonator inside. It's a spun resonator, but the hollow body is made from fiberglass material. And, it's got a wooden neck.

It has this great sound . . . just this really lonesome, far-off sound that goes inside the guitar and kind of rolls around and comes back out. It's like it's got its own echo chamber. It's like it's crying from the inside.

I didn't know how to play slide, but I knew that's what those resophonic guitars were for. So I tuned it to open D. I broke off some bottle necks until I got one that worked.

Where we live, up on the Blue Ridge Mountains, we have these incredible, intense sunrises. I'd be up in the morning, playing that guitar as the sun rose because it was the only thing that could express what I was feeling. Even though I didn't really know what I was doing. I knew about blues and I knew what was supposed to be done. I didn't have any technique, but I sure had the deepest of feelings I was trying to express musically. This instrument was able to get down in my pain and bring it up to the surface. It spoke the unspeakable.

After a couple of years of doing this every day, I realized maybe I could actually learn to play this thing, rather than just using it for a therapy tool. I wrote "Sara Jane's Tune," a slide guitar song that made me realize I had turned the corner. I knew then that I wasn't going to kill myself. I was going to live. And this funky, soulful guitar had helped lift me from the very depths of despair.

It started me playing slide guitar and now I use it in all my solo concerts. I played it in my shows with Doc Watson, and I've made a number of recordings playing the steel guitar. I practice it every day as part of what I do. I love it.

I probably have ten National Reso-Phonic guitars now. I have some great instruments. This old Airline is not a great instrument. It's just a good instrument, but it's the one that pulled me back from the edge of the abyss . . . and got me going playing slide guitar.

I credit that guitar and that man, my mother's plumber, who gave me that guitar at the right moment—the moment when I was really sinking.

It's that guitar that got me playing blues. And I still have it. I wouldn't sell it. It saved my life.

An award-winning multi-instrumentalist, storyteller, and television and radio host, **DAVID HOLT** has been performing the stories and songs of Appalachian mountaineers for more than forty-five years.

He was the musical partner of Doc Watson on stage and in the studio in the last fourteen years of Watson's life. Holt is a four-time Grammy Award winner, including two in 2002 for *Legacy*, a three-CD set with Watson that was awarded Best Traditional Folk Recording.

His television work includes PBS shows *Folkways* and *David Holt's State of Music*, TNN's *Fire On the Mountain,* and *American Music Shop*. He hosts *Riverwalk Jazz* on public radio.

Holt lives in Asheville, North Carolina.

# BILL HULLETT

In the early 1970s, I bought a 1956 Telecaster. A few years later, it was stolen out of my truck, so I went looking for a replacement. I found a Fender Nocaster for five hundred bucks. It was a great guitar.

A Nocaster has only the word "Fender" on the headstock. The first run of Fender guitars was called "Broadcaster." Gretsch drum manufacturers made a line of drums called "Broadkaster" spelled with a *k* instead of a *c*. Gretsch was an established company, and Fender was still young. Fender had made about two hundred guitars when Gretsch told them to cease using the Broadcaster name.

The story goes that Leo Fender had maybe five hundred Fender Broadcaster decals. They had only one model of guitar, so he instructed everyone to clip "Broadcaster" off the decal. When he ran out of those, he started using Telecaster decals. In the late '70s or early '80s, collectors started calling those early guitars "Nocasters."

My Nocaster was my main electric guitar for nearly thirty years. And I just flat wore it out. The neck had ditches in it, and it was almost impossible to tune. It was not a good session guitar anymore, and if I can't use a guitar, I get disgruntled with it. So I sold it for $12,500 on Ebay. That was in 2001 or 2002. I'm mainly a Tele guy, so I replaced it with other Teles and went on with life.

There's a place on the Internet called the "Telecaster Discussion Page." It's just a bunch of Tele nuts talking about guitars. I had traded e-mails with a guy in Spain, and we talked on that discussion page. He is really into vintage Teles. His name is Nacho Baños.

About two years after I sold the Nocaster, he called me out of the blue one day from Spain and said "I think your guitar is for sale in Los Angeles. I just e-mailed you some pictures." I looked at the pictures. It was my guitar.

He said he was going to buy it if I didn't want it. I didn't, so Nacho bought it for $29,000. He has a couple of Broadcasters, a couple of Nocasters, a couple of Esquires . . . he's probably got as good an early Blackguard collection as anyone on the planet. ("Blackguard" refers to the color of the pick guard Fender used on their guitars until 1954.)

In the next year or two, he writes what collectors consider the Telecaster bible. *The Blackguard* is a big coffee-table book, about an inch thick. Nacho took Teles apart and photographed them and included all this minutia about those early guitars.

He figured there were fifty-five-hundred old Blackguards made from 1950 to 1954, so the first run of the book was fifty-five-hundred copies. The old Telecasters have a serial number behind the pickup. Nacho hand-stamped a serial number on the cover of each book.

He called me again out of the blue and said, "I saved book number 0514. Come to the Dallas guitar show, and I'll give it to you. Your guitar is featured in there." The number of my Nocaster was 0514.

We met in Dallas. He gave me the book, we hung out for a day or so, and I came back home. That was that, I thought.

Then about two years ago, he e-mails me and says, "I think I'm going to have to sell 0514, so I'm taking it to the Dallas guitar show. If you'd like, come hang out for the weekend and see the guitar before I sell it."

So my wife and I went to Dallas. Nacho took us up to his room to see the Nocaster. When I picked it up, I noticed right away that the ditches weren't in the first five frets of the neck.

Nacho said, "I've got good news and bad news. The bad news is it's not my guitar anymore. The good news is I'm giving it to you." I was stunned.

He said, "I got you here on false pretenses. Number 0514 is my favorite of the entire collection and I would never get rid of it. But every time I play it, I feel guilty because it was your guitar for so long. So I made you a scratch-for-scratch, nick-for-nick duplicate."

It is identical. It has my Social Security number engraved under the pick guard and it looks like my handwriting. It even has the signature of Charlie Davis, the guy who inspected it at the Fender factory in the '50s.

I couldn't believe it. He told me that Music Craft, a company in New Jersey that makes licensed Fender necks and bodies, had contacted him after *The Blackguard* came out. They were freaked out by all the details about early Fender guitars that had never before been available. They asked if they could borrow a few of Nacho's guitars to spec out. They wanted to make a line of bodies and necks and call them "Blackguards." He said he'd do it only if they gave him three or four of the necks and bodies.

He had gotten the number 0514 body and neck from them, and he spent a year putting the finish on it, weathering it, and stripping it back. Nacho did the body and a guy in England named Clive Brown, a famous vintage restorer, did the neck.

My old Nocaster is about as beat-up and nasty as any guitar you've seen. I don't know how he was able to put all that on the "new" guitar. And it's not random stuff. It's every little nick and wear mark.

I have my Nocaster back. It's a re-creation, but it's probably a better guitar than the vintage one. It just sings like a bird.

I use it every chance I get. It's funny because I don't think of it as the copy Nacho made for me. I think of it as the guitar that's been with me for so long.

I've never heard of anyone so dedicated to make something like this. And I have never heard of anyone blessed with such a nice gift.

BILL HULLETT is a longtime session guitarist.

After leaving the Navy in 1972, he played clubs and country bars in California until he moved to Nashville in 1978.

His experience includes a combination of studio work for records and demos, live performances, and television appearances. Through the years, he has worked with many artists including George Jones, Tammy Wynette, Reba McEntire, Chet Atkins, Waylon Jennings, Willie Nelson, Martina McBride, and Vern Gosdin.

Hullett lives in Nashville.

# CORNELL HURD

I have a propensity for inexpensive guitars. I don't have anything worth more than about five hundred bucks. It's what I use to lead the band. That's what I like.

I've got a Hofner Galaxie. It's the first electric guitar I ever owned. I treasure this because my father gave it to me and because of Paul Skelton's history with it.

My father was a pilot for Philippine Airlines after World War II. All his life, he had friends in the Philippines, and he traveled there often. On one trip, he brought back three matching Hofner Galaxies for me and two of my brothers. He got a deal. Some band in the Philippines had ordered them and then not paid for them. He also brought back a little Gretch amplifier.

I was about fourteen years old and a big fan of the Ventures. I still am. I started out in 1964 as a drummer in a surf band. We were inspired by the Beach Boys' *Concert* LP, which gave us a blueprint for starting a band.

But then we saw the Beatles on *Ed Sullivan*. This was a big damn deal. Their influence permeated everything. It seemed like overnight the world completely changed and there were bands on every street.

I picked up the guitar and started my first country band in college. I went back to rock and roll in the mid-70s. What I play today combines all my previous styles, including those surf instrumentals.

One of the Hofners was stolen out of my house. Another was loaned to a saxophone player by a girl singer in my band, and it never came back. Of the guitars my father bought, this is the only one that remains.

When I went through my eBay phase, I bought three other Hofners. One is red Naugahyde and another is a not-as-cool version of the one I got from my father. The third one I shipped to my brother, Drew, who is also a musician.

The Galaxie is absolutely wonderful. It looks like a guitar you'd see in a surf band circa 1964. It's black and blond with mother-of-pearl tuning heads.

I know for a fact that in the early days of powered flight, there were fewer controls on an airplane than there are on this Hofner. It has multiple tone and volume controls and switches you can flip if you want to play a solo. It has a knob at the bottom you can turn if you want to play rhythm. This guitar has three pickups and switches that activate each one. You can turn on one pickup or any combination of three. And there's a cool mute by the bridge. You look at all the knobs and the whammy bar, and you wonder, "My God, what were they thinking?"

There are remnants of duct tape on the bottom. Before strap locks were invented, I duct-taped the strap to the body. What's not to like about this thing? Since it was my first guitar, I love it.

Years ago, a short developed in one of the jacks on the Hofner, so Paul Skelton offered to fix it for me. Paul was my lead guitarist for a long, long time. He died from lung cancer. He was a great and wonderfully creative musician. He was also a master guitar maker. At one time, he was the quality assurance manager for ESP Guitars. He also worked at Collings Guitars. He knew just about everybody in the business. He was highly regarded, and everybody in Austin loved him. His death devastated the music community.

I gave the Hofner to Skelton to fix about fifteen years ago. I say fifteen years. It may have been eighteen years. I would ask him about it and he would say, "Yeah, I'll put it together. Don't worry about that." He never got around to it, but Skelton was kind of notorious for that.

He had three of my guitars for at least fifteen years each. From 1991 until he died in 2009, that Hofner was at his house in pieces. But he gave me other guitars. For years, I played on an ESP Navigator that he gave me. I've got a Tele that Skelton made out of parts and I've also got a Kay archtop that he gave me when he was dying.

After Paul died, his wife Annie found my Hofner in pieces. I had a Hofner case for it, but I have no idea where it went. I took it to Austin Vintage Guitars and they put it together. They did a good job.

I don't remember ever playing this guitar live onstage. I wrote several of my rock-and-roll "masterpieces" from the '70s on that Hofner. I wrote "The Texas Behemoth," "The Way that You Dance," and "Heavy Breathing," which was a rock hit in San Jose. This Hofner still has some songs in it.

I never considered myself a very good guitar player or even worthy of hanging with guys who are. But Paul brought me out of that. He said, "You do what you do. And you do the one thing that you do, which is pretty good. So there's no reason why you shouldn't have a cool guitar."

I'm not here to blow anybody away with my guitar playing. I don't even have reverb on my amp because I don't like it. I think that goes back to having the soul of a drummer, to be honest.

I play rhythm guitar in my band. It's all shuffles and boogie-woogie. I'm a one-trick pony; my job is to entertain people and run the band.

Now I've got this guitar back in my life, and it's my favorite axe of all time. I love it and I cherish it.

Paul used to say you find out where you fit in with a band. He was right about that. He was an amazing, amazing man. I miss him, and I think about him every day. And *always* when I pick up the Hofner.

CORNELL HURD got his start in 1964, playing drums in a surf band in Cupertino, California. A high school talent show in 1968 changed everything for him. Hurd assembled a jug band, played guitar, and fronted the act. They played one song—and were a raging success. "I can still hear the applause" he recalls. He became a guitarist.

He began to explore country music. By 1971, he was in college in Berkeley and fronting the El Rancho Cowboys. The El Ranchos became the Mondo Hotpants Orchestra, which became the Cornell Hurd Band, an ensemble with a repertoire of Texas shuffles, swing, and rockabilly. Hurd plays rhythm guitar and is the principal songwriter. His twenty-first CD, *Boonville*, was released in 2015.

He lives in the Austin area.

# DANIEL IVANKOVICH

## AN EDUCATION IN THE BLUES

My basketball career at Northwestern University was cut short when I blew out my knee. I was in a cast from ankle to hip for six months. While I recovered, I listened to hour after hour of blues recordings.

I was sent to WNUR-FM, the radio station at Northwestern. The thinking was that, if I couldn't play basketball, maybe I could be involved in sports broadcasting. The station manager needed someone to fill in on the blues show during the summer term and offered me the job.

Around that time, I decided I needed a guitar. I bought a Supro J. B. Hutto. A year later, I picked up a fiberglass Airline. Both were made by Valco, a Chicago guitar manufacturer. I got them for almost nothing. The Supro cost me seventy-five bucks, and the Airline was about a hundred dollars. It was later called a "Jetson" because of the futuristic fins. Neither guitar came with a case, so I used a handled paper shopping bag to carry them around. Everybody laughed when I pulled out one of the red Res-O-Glas Valcos, but nobody laughed when I plugged it in. Those guitars were what was happening for me then and they were the blueprints for everything that I've played since.

I had found a blues compilation with a song by a guy named Grover Pruitt. After I played it on my radio show, I said no one had heard anything from him in thirty years and I thought he was dead. The phone rings and the guy on the line said, "Hi, this is Grover Pruitt."

Grover later showed up with his guitar and played on the radio. After that, the blues show became a way to track people down. Lil' Ed, Clarence "Gatemouth" Brown, and Lonnie Brooks all came to the studio. They loved the fact I was playing blues every Sunday for five hours. I set out to find more blues musicians.

All this time, I was taking science classes as part of my pre-med curriculum. Mr. L. C. Thurman oversaw the science labs. When I was there, I had my radio with me and lots of blues music on cassettes and 8-tracks.

He came over and said, "So you like the blues?" He said he owned the Checkerboard Lounge on Forty-Third Street on the South Side, and he invited me and my friends. We walked in and there he was behind the bar, smoking a menthol and pouring cognac. He introduced me to Buddy Guy, who was his partner at the time, and to Magic Slim, Junior Wells, Lefty Dizz, and Johnny Dollar. He was my link to all these legendary musicians. I went to the Checkerboard every week. It was like a class, and I was learning from these guys.

One of the guys I tracked down was Homesick James, Elmore James's cousin. His apartment was in the projects, and I went there to learn slide guitar. My first time there, I brought my Supro J. B. Hutto, and he said, "You just put that over there. You can play my guitar." I figured he wouldn't let me play it because Homesick was in competition with J. B. Hutto. It was like he didn't want to see that guitar. So my Supro stayed parked in the corner.

I never paid for a lesson, but I had to bring two bottles of Johnny Walker Black Label. I would have a shot or two, and he would polish off the rest of the bottle. Then he'd wheel out two Gibson lab series amps, crank them up, and start playing. Those amps must have been 130 watts each. After about twenty or thirty minutes, the police would show up and that was the end of the lesson.

I wanted to learn how to play Jimmy Reed's songs. Eddie Taylor was a legendary guitar player and Jimmy Reed's song-writing partner. All the leads, all the rhythms, and all the song structures were done by Eddie. I went to his apartment in the projects where I got lessons from him, too. In the beginning, I played his Gibson E-5. Once I got better, he let me play his Gibson ES-335. It was a kind of reinforcement, but it was also part of the bond. It felt like we were closer when he was letting me play his guitar.

After Homesick and Eddie got me started, I was on my way. They showed me songs, twelve-bar structures, and the basic patterns. They were my introduction to playing the blues. They got me deeply into Elmore James and Jimmy Reed, which was critical. The beauty of those two musicians was in the simplicity. A beginner can play Jimmy Reed. Had I started out with Otis Rush and his complex blues structures, I would have lasted all of five minutes and never played again.

This all led me to Magic Slim. Slim knew about fifteen hundred songs. He was a human jukebox. I would sit with him and he'd show me all this stuff. I ended up soloing with Slim and, ultimately, with Otis Rush.

It was a great evolution. Homesick and Eddie were like my undergrad education, Magic Slim was my Masters, and Otis Rush was my PhD.

These guys are geniuses. It just blew me away that all these people were famous and brilliant and nobody seemed to give a shit about them.

That's why I committed to making sure they had food and the resources they needed. I drove them to local clinics to get blood pressure checks and diabetic screenings. They knew they had a friend in me. I think these guys were thrilled that somebody cared about their life's work. They were very willing to impart their knowledge.

Eddie Taylor died on Christmas day in 1985 when I was in medical school. He died of uncontrolled diabetes and complications. It doesn't get any more stereotypical for a bluesman's death. He had this great wealth of knowledge and a reservoir of culture that he wanted to pass on so that he would live on. As I got older, I came to appreciate what a monster talent he was. He was phenomenal.

In a way, it was like the spoken word was passed on from the authorities. Once you receive the word, you have to pay it forward. I give back to the blues by promoting health among blues musicians. As a DJ with a syndicated blues show and a musician in a high-profile band, I have a platform to assist in keeping the blues and its musicians alive.

It's nearly impossible to miss DANIEL IVANKOVICH. At seven feet tall, he commands attention onstage as his alter ego, Chicago Slim. He studied, performed, and recorded with, among others, Eddie Taylor, Junior Wells, and Bo Diddley and was the bandleader for Otis Rush. Slim fronts the Chicago Blues All-Stars.

By day, Dr. Ivankovich is an orthopedic trauma surgeon and spine specialist. In 2010, he and his wife, Dr. Karla Ivankovich, established OnePatient Global Health Initiative. They operate three clinics in poor, underserved areas in Chicago, and Ivankovich has raised millions to expand health care services in underserved communities in the United States.

He was named 2010 "Chicagoan of the Year" by *Chicago Magazine*. In 2015, he was inducted into the Chicago Blues Hall of Fame, both as an individual and with the Chicago Blues All-Stars.

# JOHN JORGENSON

## THE DJANGO MYSTERY

My most cherished guitar is a 1942 Selmer guitar from France. These guitars are rare—only nine hundred were built between 1932 and 1952. It's worth a fair amount of money because of its rarity, but it also has an amazing sound, a very, very unusual tone. No other guitar sounds like it. It's a very delicately built instrument. I don't tour with it, but I do tend to use it often for recordings.

When I was first learning about Django Reinhardt, I found out that Selmer was the type of guitar he played. This was before the Internet. There was not that much information about Django at the time—the interest in him was more cult-like.

I bought the Selmer in Los Angeles in about 1982. At the time, I was working at Disneyland, playing bluegrass and Dixieland music. One of my friends told me that he'd seen the type of guitar that Django played at West LA Music in Westwood. That's kind of a famous music store. Stephen Stills, Jackson Browne, Bonnie Raitt, and a lot of California country-rock people bought instruments there.

To find a guitar like that one was very unusual. I said, "It can't still be there."

My friend said, "Yeah, I think it will be because it's in the back and you have to ask for it."

So I called the next day and asked if they had it, and they said they did. On my lunch hour, I got a loan from the bank. Then I called them back and said, "Please stay open for me. I'm coming on Friday afternoon and traffic might be bad from Anaheim to Westwood."

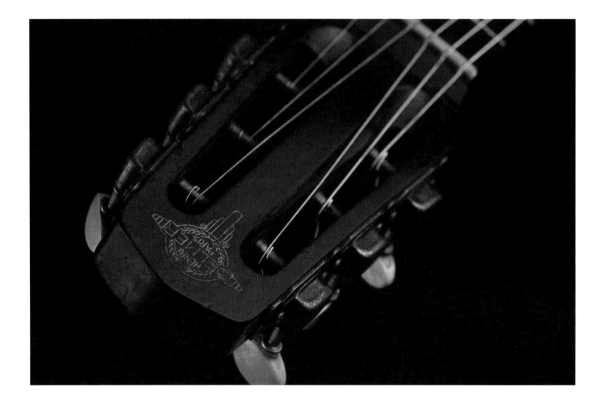

My buddy who went with me had studied a lot of Django stuff, too. When they opened the case, his eyes got really big. I made a mental note to ask him about that later.

The guitar had some cracks in the top, and I was a little iffy as to whether I should buy it. I wondered, though, when I would see another one, so I went ahead and bought it.

The salesman said there was some sort of story behind the guitar, and if I wanted to hear the story, I could give the store owner a call. So I did.

He said, "Many years ago, I got a call from a man with a very thick French accent. He said his name was Moustache and that he had a guitar that Django Reinhardt had given him. He wanted to sell it. He needed some money for a camera."

The owner thought this was a hoax, one of his friends playing a trick on him. But he told the man to bring it in. The next day, a guy with a big black mustache brought this guitar in. He was obviously from France, and he said that Django had given him the guitar for some money that he owed.

The guy at the music store didn't know if he should believe him or not, but the Selmer was worth what he wanted for it. So he bought it.

Years later, I recounted that story to a French journalist who told me that, indeed, around Paris at that time, there was a drummer and a film personality named Moustache. It's very possible Django gave him that guitar. At the very least, he was a friend of Django's.

There's a particular pattern of pick wear, where a person's fingers will rub against the face of the guitar. Willie Nelson's guitar is an extreme example. When I asked my friend why his eyes got so big when the case was opened, he said he'd seen so many pictures of Django's guitars and that the pick wear on that guitar looked exactly like what he'd seen in all the pictures.

Django had a number of guitars over the years, and it's pretty hard to tell if my guitar was one of them. But it's a cool story, and I love the instrument regardless. It's an amazing guitar.

JOHN JORGENSON is renowned for his masterful licks on the guitar. A founding member of the Desert Rose Band, he's also known for his trio the Hellecasters, as well as for his work with the gypsy jazz group the John Jorgenson Quintet.

Jorgenson joined the Elton John band in 1995 for what was supposed to be an eighteen-month gig. The job lasted six years. He has also collaborated with Bonnie Raitt, Bob Dylan, Roy Orbison, and Luciano Pavarotti. In addition to recordings by the Desert Rose Band and the Hellecasters, he has released nine solo albums.

In 2008, he shared Grammy honors for Best Country Instrumental Performance for the song "Cluster Pluck" with Brad Paisley, James Burton, Vince Gill, Albert Lee, Brent Mason, Redd Volkaert, and Steve Wariner. The Academy of Country Music named him "Guitarist of the Year" for three consecutive years.

Jorgenson lives in California.

# LAURENCE JUBER

## CLIPPED WINGS

In January 1980, Wings had just completed a UK tour, and we were on our way to Japan. Most everyone in the band went from London to Toyko, going east. I went the other way, stopping off in New York for a weekend. By coincidence, the McCartneys were also going through New York.

When I was there, I would always go down Forty-Eighth Street. It was Music Row, which was then the mecca for guitars. Now, unfortunately, it's kind of a sad shadow of its former self. Even the great Manny's Music, the historic store on that street, has closed.

Music Row was where I found a reasonably priced 1957 Les Paul Goldtop in very good condition. I just couldn't resist that guitar. It was one of the first equipped with humbuckers. The early PAF-equipped Goldtops were actually made from bodies that had been routed for the Les Paul Customs. Those tops were made from mahogany, not maple. It was a pretty unique instrument as Gibson was making Goldtops that way for only a short period of time.

With my newly acquired guitar, I flew from New York to Tokyo with the McCartneys. After a lengthy delay in Japanese immigration, we were going through customs. I was standing next to Paul when the agent opened his suitcase and discovered a bag of marijuana.

All hell broke loose. Suddenly, agents were rushing out from hidden doors, and we were escorted to the back of the customs area. All this time, I was carrying the Les Paul in its original brown Gibson case.

Because Paul had been denied a work permit in the past, everybody in the band had been warned to "vacuum their pockets" and be very cautious about going into Japan. A special dispensation had been granted him for this tour, so the bust quickly became a big deal.

While Macca was whisked off to be interrogated, I was shunted to a side room. Two customs agents entered with screwdrivers, pointing at the guitar. I wondered, were they going to seize it because I was guilty by association?

They wanted to take the guitar apart. On the Les Paul, there are two back plates—one for the control cavity and one for the switch—plus the truss rod cover. I had to prove to them that nothing was stashed there. There was a tense moment as I unscrewed the plates to demonstrate that was nothing there except the requisite wiring.

Paul was in jail for ten days and that tour, along with the rest of the year's plans, went up in smoke. The shame was that we would have been touring the US with a hit single, as the live version of "Coming Up" had been released that spring and was the number one record that summer.

I still have that Les Paul, and I've used it on multiple projects. I have great affection for that guitar.

LAURENCE JUBER was an established London studio player in 1978 when Paul McCartney asked him to join his band, Paul McCartney and Wings. Juber played lead guitar for three years in one of the most successful bands in rock music.

Following his work with McCartney, he left his native London, settling in California to reestablish his career as a successful studio musician and solo artist.

*Fingerboard Road* (2015) is his twenty-third album. Juber's guitar work can be heard on commercials and hundreds of television and movie soundtracks, including those for *Dirty Dancing*, *Good Will Hunting*, and *Pocahontas*.

He is the recipient of two Grammy Awards. "Rockestra Theme" by Paul McCartney and Wings took the award in 1980 for Best Rock Instrumental, and Juber's arrangement of "The Pink Panther Theme" won the Best Pop Instrumental in 2005.

Juber lives in Los Angeles.

# JORMA KAUKONEN

## NOT VINTAGE, JUST OLD

If I look back and pick a guitar that was particularly important in my musical development, it would be the Gibson J-50. It's a 1958 model that I bought in '59 at Pop's Music Store in Dayton, Ohio. I paid a hundred bucks for that guitar, new.

I was at Antioch College in Yellow Springs, Ohio. When I went there, I had a J-45, which I stupidly sold. I borrowed a Harmony Sovereign. I had met this great guitar player there named Ian Buchanan. He has since passed away. The Reverend Gary Davis was very influential, but it was Ian who gave me the keys to open the doors. He taught me how to fingerpick on that guitar. He was patient, and he stuck with this obnoxious kid.

There were a lot of folkies, bluegrass, and blues players around, and most had Martin D-18s or D-28s. I couldn't afford a Martin, so I gravitated toward a Gibson. When I could afford to buy my own guitar, I bought the J-50. It was the only acoustic guitar I owned for many, many years and was really the guitar that defined who I am musically today. I played it relentlessly for the next fifteen or twenty years.

I moved to San Francisco in 1962, and Jefferson Airplane got started in 1965. Through the folkie years, it was me and the J-50. I backed up Janis Joplin with that guitar. Anytime I used an acoustic on an Airplane recording, like "Embryonic Journey," it was that guitar. I used it in the beginning of Hot Tuna and on a lot of the Hot Tuna recordings. On *Live at New Orleans House*, that's the J-50. It

was with me nonstop until the '70s when I—and please forgive me for this—began playing Ovations because you could plug them in.

When the ball started rolling with the Airplane, people started coming out of the woodwork. Luthiers would say "I'd like to build a guitar for you. What are you looking for in an acoustic?" My answer was always the same: something precisely like my J-50. I already had exactly what I needed or wanted.

I like getting guitars off the assembly line. Not that I don't like custom shop stuff, and I'm not averse to modifying—don't get me wrong. I guess I'm struggling to redeem my working-class roots. I have nothing against fancy guitars. But there's something I like about buying a stock guitar new and having it break in to me and my playing.

All of us acoustic guitar guys play plugged in these days. I retired the J-50 a number of years ago because I didn't want to do what was necessary in order to amplify it. It's starting to get fragile with age, but it doesn't just sit there. I pick it up and play it. It needs to know it's still loved.

You pick up a guitar and certain ones just say, "You need to write a song in D major, and I'm the guitar to help you do that." The old J-50 led me to my song "Genesis" and, in a way, wrote the music for me.

Today that guitar lives in our Psylodelic Museum at the Fur Peace Ranch in Darwin, Ohio. I haven't played it in a while. I'll go back to it and that sound will come out—the old mahogany sound. And, of course, it has that delightful ancient guitar smell we all love so much. That guitar is more than fifty years old, but to me, it's not vintage. It's just old.

For many musicians, seven years in a band as legendary as Jefferson Airplane would be the apex of a career. For JORMA KAUKONEN, it was just a start.

He helped form the Airplane in the early '60s, his guitar playing instrumental in creating a sound that led to critical and commercial success and induction into the Rock and Roll Hall of Fame.

With Airplane bassist and friend Jack Casady, Kaukonen formed Hot Tuna as a side project. It became his main gig when he left the Airplane in 1972. The band has recorded more than twenty albums and continues to tour regularly.

In an impressive solo career, Kaukonen has released a dozen albums, including the 2015 *Ain't in No Hurry*.

He also established Fur Peace Ranch Guitar Camp in southeastern Ohio, where, since 1989, thousands of musicians have been instructed by Kaukonen and other prominent musicians.

He lives in Ohio.

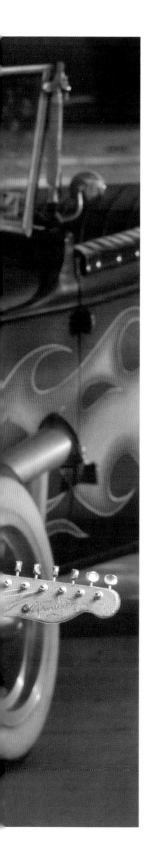

# BILL KIRCHEN

## THREE NEW HEADS AND FIVE NEW HANDLES

I'd like to tell you about the first Telecaster I ever played. And, for at least two decades, it was the only Telecaster I played.

I had discovered country music—specifically, the Bakersfield twang. I loved Buck Owens, and I knew his guitar player was Don Rich. I loved Merle Haggard, and his guitar player then was Roy Nichols. And I loved the rockabilly I heard by Ricky Nelson, and the guitar player on those records was James Burton.

At the time, I had a Gibson SG. But when I realized they all played Telecasters, I knew I wanted a Tele.

The Commander Cody band had broken up. George Frayne had gone off to teach art at Oshkosh, Wisconsin. The guy I had bought the guitar from, John Tichy, had left to get his doctorate in engineering. And I moved from Ann Arbor to San Francisco to see what I could do.

I wasn't making much money. I had to scrape together what I had to get to California. I couldn't make a living right off the bat playing music, so I got a job as a motorcycle messenger to get by. There would be three or four of us messengers sitting on the bench, waiting for the next run. I got to talking with this guy about guitars. I think Pete Townshend had just come through town playing, and smashing up, a Gibson SG. This guy wanted to get a Gibson and he had a Tele. I had a Gibson and wanted to get a Tele. So I said, "Man, let's trade."

We traded across the board. This was about 1968.

Shortly after I traded for the Tele, I convinced the Commander Cody band to come out West. George Frayne was tired of teaching, and I talked everybody into moving to California. The rest is history.

I cut "Hot Rod Lincoln," a top ten hit for Commander Cody, on that Telecaster. I used it on all the Cody albums, and I was playing the Tele probably on 99 percent of the live shows I did.

I've only recently taken it off the road. It used to be a sunburst. Now you'd be hard-pressed to find any of the sunburst on the front. You can still see some of it on the back.

It's like the story of the guy who has had the same axe in his family. He says, "Yeah, I've had this axe for seven generations. It's had three new heads and five new handles!" I'm like that. The only thing left of my Telecaster is the stick of the neck, the body of the plank, and a decal that says "Fender." The only metal that's left is the six-string ferrules that the strings go through.

Other than that, everything on that guitar—every wire, every fret, every knob, every screw, every pot—has been replaced many, many times. I eventually changed everything on it, but only if I needed to. There's a hole on the Tele that's almost a quarter-inch deep, just below the bridge plate, from where I've rested my pinky finger for decades.

Now bear in mind, the guitar was probably from the '50s, but it looked brand new when I got it. We could never figure out if it was a factory refinish. Maybe it was a new neck—we never did know. But everything about it, the serial number and the pickup, it all pointed to being from the '50s. I bought the SG for a hundred, and I'm sure he hadn't paid much more than that for the Tele. There were a lot of great people playing them, but it didn't have this collectible thing yet.

Once I got the Tele, that was the last day job I ever had that wasn't about music.

As an alum of Commander Cody and His Lost Planet Airmen, BILL KIRCHEN will forever be associated with the group's hit song, "Hot Rod Lincoln," which features his distinctive Telecaster licks. The band was among the pioneers of the country-rock sound.

Kirchen maintains a busy schedule touring internationally and playing his signature mix of rockabilly, country, and blues. In a nod to his songs about long-haul truck drivers, he calls this sound "dieselbilly."

In addition to recording and touring with his band, Too Much Fun, the songwriter has recorded with, among others, Nick Lowe, Elvis Costello, Arlen Roth, Redd Volkaert, and Sammy Hagar.

Kirchen can also be found, with his ever-present Telecaster, teaching at Jorma Kaukonen's Fur Peace Ranch in Ohio.

Kirchen lives in Texas.

# SONNY LANDRETH

## THE STRAT UNDER THE BED

My friend, Dave Ranson, bought a '65 Strat. This was in the early '70s. He was playing guitar a lot. Hell, he was playing better than I was back then.

One night, we played this gig north of Lafayette. It was rough out there. There were clubs with gambling, strippers . . . the works.

The particular place we played wasn't quite like that, but it was pretty funky. The crowd hated us. When we went to get paid at the end of the night, the guy begrudgingly paid us all of $100. He was surrounded by his cronies, and it was like they all wanted to beat us up.

Long story short: I left the club thinking Dave got his guitar and he thought I got it.

Maybe a week went by and Dave calls me up. He said, "I wanna come by and get my Strat."

"What do you mean? Don't you have it?"

"I don't have it. Don't you have it?"

We went back to the club and, of course, the owner said, "No, I didn't see any guitar."

There wasn't anything we could do.

It was one of the lowest points ever for me. It was his guitar, not mine. I felt bad about that for a long, long time.

All that happened in 1972 or 1973. Fast forward to 1982. We were playing with a band called the Bayou Rhythms. One day we were waiting to play a gig, backing up Zachary Richard. We were hanging out and eating gumbo when a friend tells us that he'd heard about a Strat for sale by the owner of that same club.

Dave and I just looked at each other. We had put it behind us and moved on, but suddenly we both felt like something extraordinary was about to happen.

I had played in that club over the years in other bands. The owner got to know me and he had completely forgotten about that first gig from way back.

I called him and said, "I hear you got a guitar for sale."

"Yeah, you really should check it out."

Dave and I go there and he brings it out and says, "It's a really nice guitar." He said it was his kid's guitar. Of course, we looked at it and knew it was *the* guitar. There was an identifying mark on the back of the neck, and we had the serial number, which checked out.

I said, "There's only one problem."

"What's that?"

"This is Dave's guitar. This is the one we left here nine years ago. You said you didn't have it, but it turns out you did."

You should have seen the look on his face. He started backpedaling. "No! A salesman came through here with that guitar." And he goes into this bizarre story of how he got it, which made no sense at all. His girlfriend was standing there and even she didn't believe it. She said, "You say the salesman just *left* the guitar here?"

We started walking to the door. "We'll go to the police and see what they say."

He said, "They won't do anything."

I said, "Let's go find out."

This guy was on parole. I'm not sure what had happened, but he went to prison. When he got out, he went back to running his bar.

As we walk toward the door, the price starts dropping. He started out at $300. Then it was $250 . . . $175. By the time we got to the front door, it was $100.

We went to the police station and reported what had happened. The detective said, "I know him. I'm his parole officer." We're telling him the story, and he's filling out the forms. I could tell he was getting impatient. "That's enough!" he said. "I'm just gonna go get that damned guitar!"

"Can we come along?"

He said, "No, you stay here."

So we waited at the police station, and, sure enough, in about an hour, he came back with Dave's Strat. He said that when he pulled up, the guy was waiting for him with the guitar. He didn't even have to get out of the squad car. The guy just walked out and handed it to him.

We were elated. We drove back to Lafayette to our neighborhood bar. All our buddies were there. We started buying Peppermint Schnapps. I had never had one in my life, but I think I had ten that night.

Apparently, the guitar had been under the bed all those years. It was in great condition.

I offered to buy it from Dave way back, but even back then, the value kept going up. Dave just wants me to play it anytime I want, and bless his heart for letting me. It's absolutely the best-sounding Strat I've ever played.

Called the "King of Slydeco," SONNY LANDRETH has a bluesy, rock-infused way of playing slide guitar that is all his own. While his right hand picks, slaps, and taps the strings, his left hand frets notes and plays chords behind the slide.

As a teen, he soaked up the musical influences of zydeco and the Deep South, eventually joining Clifton Chenier and his Red Hot Louisiana Band. His second solo album, *Down in Louisiana,* led to his work with John Hiatt in the studio and in Hiatt's band, The Goners. He has also recorded with, among others, John Mayall, Johnny Winter, and Buckwheat Zydeco. Eric Clapton has called Landreth one of the most advanced, and most under-appreciated, guitar players in the world.

His 2003 album, *The Road We're On*, was nominated for a Grammy. His twelfth record, *Bound by the Blues*, was released in 2015.

Landreth lives in Louisiana.

# JACK LAWRENCE

DOC'S MARTIN

I have a 1945 model D-18 Martin. It was given to me by a guy I worked with for twenty-seven years, Doc Watson.

He bought this guitar in 1963 and used it on a good many of his Vanguard Records in the 1960s. He used it on records like *Home Again!* He used it on the record he did with Flatt and Scruggs, *Strictly Instrumental*. And he used it on *Doc Watson on Stage*, a record that is a bible for aspiring flatpickers.

Every year, Doc and I played at a place called The Down Home in Johnson City, Tennessee. We usually played there the weekend before Christmas.

The first time I played there with him in 1985, I picked Doc up, went to The Down Home, played, and came back to his house, where I stayed the night.

The next morning, I got up early and went downstairs to his music room. Behind the stereo in the corner, under about a half-inch of dust, was this old Martin guitar. I picked it up and dusted it off. The bridge was coming off and it had maybe two or three strings on it. I recognized that guitar as the D-18 I had seen on record covers.

When Doc came into the room, I was tapping on it to check for loose braces.

"What are you doing?" he asked.

I said, "I found this old guitar in the corner, and I believe it still has some music in it. You ought to fix it up."

"That guitar is road dead," he said. "I wore that thing out. I took it to Africa . . . it's been all around the world. It was in a car accident and was thrown out of the car and out of the case on the side of the road. It's just road dead."

"I think I could probably fix it."

"It's not really worth anything." he said. "One of these days, I'll just give it to you."

It didn't happen that weekend.

A pattern developed. Every year, I'd pick Doc up, we'd go to Johnson City, do The Down Home, and come back to his house. I'd get up in the morning, go downstairs to the music room, and pick that guitar up. I'd sniff the sound hole, bang on the top, and tell Doc it had music in it.

Then he'd say, "One of these days, I'll just give that to you." This went on for four, maybe five years.

Finally, he said, "Aw hell, just take it. But I want to keep the Grover Rotomatic tuning machines that are on it because that's the only thing that's worth anything on the guitar."

So I took those off and left them with him. And I took it home.

I did most of the work on it myself. It was in worse shape than I thought. I put it on my workbench and spent a couple of months tinkering around with it. I had to replace some wood underneath the bridge, put a new bridge plate inside, fix a couple of cracks, refret it, that sort of thing.

I'd been telling Doc all those years that it still had some music in it. And after a few months, I got it back to playing music. It still had that dryness of tone and the warmth that I remember on those old Doc records from the '60s.

The first time I took it out, we were doing some recording sessions for a couple of Doc's records. This was in 1989 or 1990. We were doing sessions for a record called *On Praying Ground* and another one called *My Dear Old Southern Home*. I used that guitar on those sessions. It had come full circle and was recorded again on Doc Watson records—only with me playing it.

I handed it to Doc and he strummed it a few times. And I could tell by the look on his face that he was thinking I was right—he should have gotten this fixed. And he said, "There *was* some music left in this old guitar. This is really playing good and sounds good. It's got the tone that I remember."

I said, "Well, yeah, maybe one of these days I'll give it to you."

He always said that he was never going to do anything with that guitar, and he was just happy that I was able to put it back together. I used it on the road for a few years with him. It's old and fragile. It's temperamental. But I flew all over the world with it, playing it at Doc's shows.

It's a very special instrument to me. As far as I'm concerned, it's a piece of history.

JACK LAWRENCE met Doc Watson and his son, Merle, in the early 1980s, an introduction that led to a long and fruitful musical partnership.

Lawrence was a seasoned veteran, playing country, bluegrass, and rock and roll going back to 1971. While playing with Joe Smothers in a folk duo, he was introduced to the Watsons. Upon Merle's retirement from touring with his father, Lawrence was asked to join the elder Watson on the road. It was a musical relationship that would endure for twenty-seven years.

Other musical partnerships include stints with the New Deal String Band and the Bluegrass Alliance. Lawrence has recorded solo albums and albums with Watson, including the Grammy-winning *On Praying Ground*.

The "flatpicking powerhouse," as he's been called, continues to write, record, and tour. His most recent album, *Arthel's Guitar*, was released in 2013.

Lawrence lives in North Carolina.

# GREG LEISZ

## TWENTY BUCKS WELL SPENT

In 1970, I bought my first lap steel, a 1954 Fender Champion student model. It cost me sixty bucks and that included the matching Fender Champ amp. I learned to play it by playing along with Hank Williams records.

My second lap steel guitar was a Rickenbacker Electro model. These were the first commercially available models of the electric guitar from the early 1930s. It's commonly called a "frying pan" because of the shape. It has a small round body with a long neck, and it's made from a single piece of cast aluminum. This model was an A25, which refers to the twenty-five-inch scale length.

I had no idea what it was when I bought it in 1973. Two teenagers brought it into a music store called Coast Music in Orange County. I had just started playing pedal steel, and I was there checking one out. They asked if I knew anyone who'd be interested in buying it. I said I would, but all I had on me was twenty dollars. They both lit up like candles. "Twenty dollars! Really?" I think they wanted the money to buy some pot. Back then, twenty dollars could buy a good-sized bag.

I took it home, plugged it into a Fender Twin Reverb, and heard this beautiful, big, open sound. It was the first time I'd really heard a Rickenbacker steel guitar with a horseshoe magnet pickup.

In 1975, I took my frying pan on the road when I was playing with John Stewart. On that tour, we flew and checked all our gear, but I never checked the frying pan. I always carried it with me. Then in Chicago, I left it in the trunk of a cab at the airport. When I got back to LA, I contacted the cab company. Luckily, they had it and shipped it back to me. That could have been the end of my relationship with the instrument almost before it started.

A couple of years after I bought the lap steel, the pickup began to cut out and not work properly. I asked Richard Smith, a friend who knew a lot about old instruments, about repairing it. He recommended I take it to Doc Kaufmann. Doc was Leo Fender's original partner.

He looked at it and immediately saw the problem. There's a cavity in the body where the pickup fits in from the top. To access the internal wiring, you have to take the entire pickup assembly out. Doc fixed it, but in order to make it easier to repair in the future, he cut two jagged access holes in the back of the body and covered them with plastic plates screwed into the aluminum. Doc looked at it like an engineer. He saw a flaw in the design and improved it. A legendary pioneer in electric guitar history fixed my frying pan.

The guitar worked great for ten or fifteen years until it started cutting out again. Sadly, Doc had passed away by then, so I took it to Seymour Duncan who repaired it using Doc's improved design to access the problem.

The first time I played the frying pan on a commercially released record was in 1976. I was with a band called Funky Kings. That record had elements of R&B, folk, and country, and the frying pan was an important part of the band's sound. At the time, I was heavily influenced by David Lindley's approach to the lap steel with Jackson Browne. In the '80s, I played it extensively on tour and in the studio with Dave Alvin.

I've more or less retired it from touring, but in 2013, I took it out on tour with Eric Clapton. If someone says, "I need a lap steel on this session," I automatically bring it. When I pick it up to play, someone usually comments on it. It's a conversation piece.

The frying pan is now twice as old as when I got it in 1973. I've used it for more than forty years on tour and in the studio. It has a unique sound and tends to stand out in recordings. Besides being a damn good investment of twenty bucks, my frying pan had a lot to do with giving me a voice on the lap steel. I have no doubt.

Over a career covering more than four decades, multi-instrumentalist GREG LEISZ has worked with an impressive array of artists in rock and roll, pop, jazz, and roots music.

The musician was honored with a Lifetime Achievement Award for Instrumentalist from the Americana Music Association in 2010. That same year, he was awarded a Grammy for his contribution to Ray LaMontagne's *God Willin' & the Creek Don't Rise*.

Among his producer credits are Lucinda Williams's *Down Where the Spirit Meets the Bone*, Dave Alvin's *Ash Grove* and *King of California*, and Chuck Prophet's *Let Freedom Ring*.

Leisz has toured with Joni Mitchell, Joe Cocker, Emmylou Harris, Ray LaMontagne, k.d. lang, Bill Frisell, Jackson Browne, and Eric Clapton. His recording credits include Willie Nelson, Kris Kristofferson, Daft Punk, Bonnie Raitt, Bon Iver, Bruce Springsteen, Jackson Browne, Randy Newman, the Eagles, and Eric Clapton.

He lives in California.

# JOHN LEVENTHAL

## ONE GUITAR, ONE THOUSAND GIGS

I was a bit of a late bloomer in that I didn't get my first electric guitar until my senior year in college. I was twenty-one.

I was going to go to law school, but I decided to take a year off to play in a band with some friends—including Robbie Kaplan, a childhood friend from New York. He was the first musician I knew who shared my eclectic tastes in music. We loved everything from the Beatles and the Stones to Howlin' Wolf, Miles Davis, Wes Montgomery, Doc Watson, and Merle Haggard. It just ran the gamut.

We moved to Colorado and started a band called Fairplay. We stuck it out for a couple of years, but eventually I realized I needed to be in New York if I wanted to get serious about making it as a musician. The band was struggling, and I gave up on it. Robbie stayed, and I moved back to New York.

About four months later, he died in an accident. A good friend of ours was with him when he died. He called me immediately. In the fog of our grief, we decided it would be best if I told Robbie's parents because it became apparent that they wouldn't be told for a few hours. At the time, it seemed like the right thing to do.

Telling his parents was one of the hardest things I've ever had to do in this world, but, of course, nothing compared to what his family experienced.

Robbie had a 1970 Telecaster and I had a 1966 Gibson 335. I was never happy with that guitar and had secretly coveted his Telecaster. A few months after he passed, his parents gave it to me.

That Telecaster has always been special to me—and not only because it belonged to my friend. It's special because I've used it to do what he and I had always fantasized about as kids: making music with great musicians. It's a powerful feeling.

I used it for a long time, from 1977 until about 2002. I must have done close to a thousand gigs with that Telecaster. I just wore it out. It's had three, if not four, fret jobs. Finally a luthier told me that it couldn't be re-fretted anymore. There's not a thing on it that's original except the body, neck, knobs, and control plate. I put a mini humbucker in the neck position because Marc Shulman, another childhood friend, had a guitar with one and I liked the way that sounded.

Before either of us accomplished much of anything, Jim Lauderdale and I were good friends. I produced and co-wrote most of the songs on Jim's first album, *Planet Of Love*. Most people have never heard of it, but it was big for me because a lot of those songs got covered by other artists, such as George Strait and Vince Gill, and that basically helped buy the house my family and I now live in.

That album had Robbie's Telecaster all over it.

I still think of Robbie. I doubt there's been a month gone by in my life since he passed away when I haven't thought about him.

I learned to be a musician on that guitar. I found my voice as a player. I could never imagine parting with it.

I never did go to law school.

In music circles, JOHN LEVENTHAL is best known as a Grammy Award–winning producer, songwriter, and musician.

The list of artists he's worked with in country, folk, and blues is long. It includes Marc Cohn, Michelle Branch, Elvis Costello, the Tedeschi Trucks Band, Bruce Hornsby, Willie Nelson, Jackson Browne, Charlie Haden, Levon Helm, and William Bell.

Shawn Colvin and he co-wrote the hit single "Sunny Came Home," which won 1998 Grammy Awards for Song of the Year and Record of the Year. His work with Rosanne Cash for her 2014 album, *The River & The Thread*, won the 2015 Grammy for Best Americana Album. Their song, "A Feather's Not a Bird," won Grammy Awards for Best American Roots Song and Best American Roots Performance.

He lives in New York City with his wife, Rosanne Cash.

# DAVE MALONE

## THE $80 TELECASTER

I grew up in Edgard, Louisiana. In 1968, I was fifteen years old and in a band called the Family Dog. I was playing a crappy, no-name guitar that belonged to my older brother's friend.

The rhythm guitar player, Tim Pedeaux, was going to school in New Orleans during the week. He saw a classified ad in the paper there that said "Fender guitar, a hundred dollars." I asked him to check it out. He called me and said it was fine. We talked the lady down, so it only cost me eighty dollars for a 1956 Telecaster.

Frankly, Telecasters were not popular at the time. Everyone wanted Stratocasters. There were no videos then, and I didn't get music magazines. I didn't know, for instance, that Jeff Beck and Jimmy Page were using Telecasters or Esquires in the Yardbirds. I did know that James Burton, who played behind Ricky Nelson and Elvis Presley, played a Telecaster.

Nobody knew much of anything about vintage stuff. In fact, it wasn't even vintage then. I stripped the body and refinished it four or five times when I was still living in the country. I've painted it all different colors, but the thing has since been put back to the original whitish butterscotch finish. It wasn't a pristine vintage instrument. But I loved it.

I couldn't wait to get the hell out of Edgard and join my older brother in New Orleans where there was a music scene and stuff to do. I finished high school early and moved there with my Telecaster. That guitar was meant to be with me, and I'll tell you why.

I had always been enamored with Les Pauls. It just so happened I was living in uptown New Orleans and this guy, whose name I don't recall, had an old Les Paul. We were just jamming and we swapped guitars. We both said, "Wow, this is great!" So we made the decision we'd trade guitars.

The very next day, I was playing the Les Paul and I thought, I really don't like this thing. What the hell did I do? I was trying to think of ways to get my guitar back without looking like an asshole when he calls me and says he wants to trade back. I swear to God.

When I told my friends about swapping my Telecaster, they all said, "You moron! I can't believe you traded this guitar away."

But I got it back.

At one point in the mid-1970s, the metal pieces were all rusty and the wood was beat up. My drummer Jim Scheurich and his brother Rick, the band manager, offered to pay to have it refinished.

They knew I was a Clarence White nut and that I could not figure out how the hell he played the stuff he played. I finally caught wind that he had a device on his guitar that was bending the string like a pedal steel guitar. I had never seen one. I had only heard him on records.

They ended up taking my old Telecaster and sending it off to California. They got it refinished, refurbished, and refretted. It was very generous. I still can't believe they did it. It was a very cool surprise.

They had it finished in a solid black. They also had a B-string bender installed by Gene Parsons. I was actually the first person east of Colorado to have a B-Bender. I got the Telecaster back and it was like a whole new ballgame.

Installing the B-Bender essentially made it somewhat of a hollow body. If it had been a pristine vintage guitar, that installation would have de-valued it by about half. But nobody thought that way back then. And it wasn't a pristine vintage instrument. I had re-finished it several times. I had changed the pickups and put different tuners on it. I still have all the original pieces.

On two different occasions I pulled boneheaded stunts with this guitar. The first time I was getting divorced from my first wife and living on a friend's couch. I opened the trunk of my car and put the amp in, but I left the guitar sitting in the street outside their apartment. When I remembered, I drove back and, of course, it was gone. I just freaked out.

I happened to have a piece of paper in the case with the phone number of the couple I was staying with. The next day, this guy called. He knew who I was from the Radiators. He explained he was walking down Prytania Street and saw a guitar case with no cars around. So he picked it up, carried it home, opened it, and found that phone number.

I gave him some guitar lessons for saving my Telecaster.

Another time, we were playing a club called the Dream Palace on Frenchman Street. It was probably three-thirty in the morning. The same damned thing happened. I opened the trunk, put my stuff in the car, and left the guitar on the street. I got almost all the way home and it hit me like a bolt of lightning. My guitar!

I whipped the car around and I drove all the way back—and I'm talking like forty-five minutes at that point—and damned if it wasn't still sitting there on the side of the road.

So I was a lot more careful after that. It's impossible to explain, but that guitar means so much to me. It's family, you know?

DAVE MALONE fronted the New Orleans rock-and-roll band, the Radiators, for more than thirty years. *OffBeat* magazine described the band as New Orleans's longest-running and most successful rock band. The Radiators were inducted into the Louisiana Music Hall of Fame in 2011.

Fronting a legendary band for forty-five-hundred shows and fifteen albums would be a career for most people. For Malone, the end of the Radiators marked a beginning. Relentless touring had prevented the band members from pursuing projects with other musicians. When they disbanded, Malone put together a new band with two Radiators bandmates and members of other New Orleans bands. Raw Oyster Cult was born.

With a fiercely loyal Radiators fan base, Raw Oyster Cult is a vehicle to continue performing Radiators songs, as well as new music, written or co-written by Malone.

He lives in Louisiana.

# ROB MCNELLEY

## MORE THAN JUST A GUITAR

I grew up in Columbus, Ohio, and my father was a musician. He was in McGuffey Lane, a country-rock band, on Atco Records.

I started playing guitar when I was eight. I never took lessons. I just learned from him and from the musicians I was around.

Back in 1981, my dad bought a '55 Fender Telecaster from Gruhn Guitars in Nashville. I was eleven years old. I remember the night he brought it home and showed it to me. The second he opened the case, I just completely fell in love with that guitar. It's a white-blond Tele with a white pick guard. It just looked so cool.

There's not a lot of finish on the neck. It's been played and played and played. He brought it home and I played it all the time. In fact, when it was time for him to go on the road, he'd have to find the guitar because I would hide it. I'd put it under my bed or somewhere where, hopefully, he'd forget it and not take it with him. Of course, he always found it.

He passed away when I was seventeen.

I got all his guitars, but the Tele was missing. I didn't know what happened to it. I didn't know where it was.

Years later, in 1995, when I moved to Nashville, I was talking with a friend of my dad's, and I asked him about that Tele. He told me it belonged to Paul Worley. He's a famous producer in Nashville. At the time, he was head of A&R at Sony Records. He had produced two of my dad's records back in the '80s and, I guess, he bought the guitar from my dad.

My friend was working for Worley at the time. He took me up to his office and introduced us. I was just fresh in town and I didn't have any money. I said, "Mr. Worley, I understand you have that Tele. I know it's in good hands, but if you ever decide you'd like to get rid of it, please let me know. I know I probably couldn't pay you what it's worth . . ." At the time, a '55 Tele would have been worth anywhere from five thousand to eight thousand dollars, and I just didn't have that kind of money.

A few months went by. One day, our mutual friend, Cliff Audretch, calls me and says, "I don't know what you're doing tonight, but if you don't have plans, stop by."

So I went over to his house, and when I walked in, he just pointed to a guitar case on the floor. I opened it and there it was. I knew exactly what it was. It was just like I was eleven years old again.

"Paul called me," said Audretch, "and told me to go over to his house. He told me where it was and to get it. He wants you to have it."

I have pictures of myself playing this guitar when I was a kid. I used to open for my dad at festivals. I have pictures of myself playing it on stage when I was twelve.

I've played on some records for Paul, and every time I bring that guitar, we sit down and play it. It always leads to another story about my dad. It's just this really cool thing. We've got this link through this guitar.

How do you show your appreciation for something like that? I don't know if there is a way . . . He's given me something back that's irreplaceable. It's more than just a guitar. It was my dad's guitar.

ROB MCNELLEY got to Nashville in 1995, moving there from his native Columbus, Ohio.

He started out touring with artists such as Tinsley Ellis, Allison Moorer, Lee Ann Womack, and Wynonna Judd. In 2002, he began touring and recording with Delbert McClinton, and he played on McClinton's *Cost of Living*, which won the Grammy for Best Contemporary Blues Album in 2005.

He has also worked with, among others, Buddy Guy, B. B. King, Toby Keith, Montgomery Gentry, Al Anderson, Randy Houser, Kellie Pickler, and Lady Antebellum, as well as with producers Tom Dowd and Paul Worley.

McNelley lives in Nashville.

# LISA MORALES

This guitar was a rare find. I bought it at the guitar show in Houston in 1995. At the time, Gibson wasn't making J-200 Jr. guitars anymore. They are now, but they weren't then.

It was perfect for me because a Jumbo just dwarfs me. It kind of looks like the Everly Brothers model, only it's blond. The funny thing is, I'd never wanted a blond guitar, but for me, it's always been about how the guitar sounds and not how it looks.

Back then, my sister Roberta and I had a band called Sisters Morales. In 1995, we got a record deal with RCA. We flew into Nashville to make our record, and when we arrived, I went to get the van while everyone else collected the luggage. When I pulled up, everybody looked at me like I had lost my dearest friend. "It's bad," Roberta said. My husband told me that a forklift had gone through the back of my guitar.

The hole in the guitar was small compared to the hole in the case. The Southwest Airlines people took one look at it and said they would totally take care of it. They paid for the guitar. They went above and beyond in the way they handled the situation and the way they treated me.

Still, we were about to record for a major label and the one thing that is comfortable in my hands was messed up.

Lucky for us, we had become friends with John Jennings, Mary Chapin Carpenter's producer at the time, and Steve Buckingham, a label exec at Sony. They were both really close to the guys at Gibson.

We called them because we wanted to know where we could borrow some guitars. John said Mike McGuire with the Gibson Custom Shop could fix mine. The people at Gibson also lent me some guitars.

Mike took every single splinter and put that guitar completely back together. It was a Gibson guitar and they were going to do right by it. They were really honorable cats. Their workmanship is something to be reckoned with. Fact is, that guitar was always a little too trebly until they fixed it. Then the sound ended up being really nice, full and round.

The next year, we were playing the Houston Westheimer Arts Festival. That festival is a blast. After our show, our drummer, Rick Richards, and bass player, Larry Evans, had to rush out and play other gigs. I wanted to help them load up so they could get on the road. I grabbed my guitar and put it under the stage to keep it out of the way. I was so busy helping them and then autographing merchandise that I forgot all about my guitar. It wasn't until that night or the next morning that I realized I didn't have it.

I called the festival and they said they would call the sound company. They called back and said there was no guitar found, but they gave me the phone number for the sound guy. I called him and he said he hadn't seen it.

This was before Facebook, so I asked friends to put the word out. Houston is a real community town, so the word got out pretty fast.

I called Dennis, who worked at the Guitar Center. He said some guy came in and looked at a guitar that fit the description of mine. He was boasting, saying, "My buddy just got a guitar like this."

Dennis told him, "That's Lisa Morales's guitar and you'd better get your buddy to call here right now and get the guitar back to her."

Turns out, it was the sound man who had nabbed it. He called me and said, "Hey, you won't believe it, but I *found* your guitar!" All this happened about a week later.

Sometime later, we were doing a gig outside of Houston and the same sound guy came up to me. He said, "Hey, how's it going? I'm the one who returned your guitar!"

To tell you the truth, he was terrible at sound.

So far that guitar has had a couple of lives. I've kept it and I still play it. It just keeps going.

LISA MORALES was taught by her grandmother to play the piano at age five. By seven, she was learning guitar, and by ten, she was writing songs. "When I was fourteen, my dad died, and I wrote a lot more. I had just purchased my first steel-string guitar, and I sat in a room and wrote and played until my fingers bled."

After college, she worked as a solo performer, later partnering with her sister, Roberta, to form the Sisters Morales. Together for more than twenty years, the band played a mix of pop, rock, and Americana, singing some songs in English and others in Spanish. Their recordings include *Ain't No Perfect Diamond* (1997) and *Talking to the River* (2006).

Morales released her solo debut, *Beautiful Mistake,* in 2011. In addition to writing and performing, she has also produced for Hayes Carll.

She lives in San Antonio, Texas.

# SCRAPPY JUD NEWCOMB

## A GOOD KIND OF WORN

This guitar is a real favorite of mine, and I feel very lucky to have it. It was made by Stephen Wise, who is an Austin guitar builder. It has a butterfly inlay on the headstock. I don't know if he's still using that, but it was the Wise logo initially. It's not a Martin. It's not a Gibson. It's a guitar made by a guy who had made fewer than ten guitars at that point.

As I understand it, this guitar was the eighth one that Wise made. I think it was modeled after a D-28, but it has unique dimensions. I don't think I've ever found a pickup that does it justice. Played acoustically and mic'd up, it has a unique thing going.

Champ Hood, Warren Hood's father, gave this guitar to me when we were both playing with Toni Price. I was pretty young at the time. Casper Rawls was in that band, too. It was an acoustic band, but I didn't have an acoustic guitar with a pickup in it that was good enough for playing at gigs. I would borrow guitars from friends for a couple of months at a time.

Champ said, "I've got this old guitar that you're welcome to use for a while." David Ball got it when he was in Uncle Walt's Band with Champ and Walter Hyatt. Somehow Champ ended up with it, and he ended up just giving it to me. I think that was in '94.

It was my one and only acoustic for many, many years. It was broken in by the time I got it and that's because Uncle Walt's Band played mostly acoustically. They were a premier acoustic band in Austin in the mid-'70s through the mid-'80s. They would play

medium-size listening rooms with no PA. Sometimes, they might have had one mic in kind of a bluegrass style. To be heard, and because a lot of that stuff had a pretty lively swing, Champ would play it pretty hard. There's a lot of wear on it. A lot of good wear.

The cosmetics of my guitars have never been a big consideration of mine. I know there was one major repair when it was damaged on the road, and on the top there's another piece of wood that has been patched in.

It's very sweet sounding, not shrill at all. It doesn't have a booming, low end. It's got a sound like a bell.

I remember playing a gig after I'd had it for probably ten years. One of Champ's old girlfriends was there, and she had seen him play it in the early '80s. This was probably fifteen years later. She said, "I was so glad to see that guitar. I knew it immediately when I heard it." It doesn't sound like any other guitar. After Champ's passing, this guitar became even dearer to me.

One of the bands I'm very lucky to play in is called the Resentments. It's an acoustic-based band that's been together for about fifteen years. It started as a loose collection of sidemen and songwriters. Over the years, it coalesced into a regular lineup. And before we knew it, we were making records and going on the road. Stephen Bruton was one of the main guys who started the band. He was one of my oldest friends and a real mentor to me. He died a few years back.

I played this same guitar in that band. I have some great memories associated with it. When I play music, I feel a connection to old friends and bandmates, people who helped me and taught me all kinds of things.

I have so many great memories of playing with friends who are gone and a great many who are still here. All those gigs are still in this guitar.

A long-time Austin, Texas, musician, SCRAPPY JUD NEWCOMB is a journeyman. The guitarist is ubiquitous.

He can be seen with the Resentments in the band's long-running Sunday residency at the Saxon Pub and with Johnny Nicholas and Hellbent. For twenty years, he was part of the late Ian McLagan's Bump Band. Newcomb was also a member of Toni Price's band for seven years.

Newcomb has worked with many other musicians in the studio and on the road, including Jon Dee Graham, Stephen Bruton, Patty Griffin, Walter Tragert, Matt the Electrician, Slaid Cleaves, Bob Schneider, and Bobby Whitlock and CoCo Carmel. His producing credits include Cleaves, Beaver Nelson, and Loose Diamonds.

With three solo albums to his credit since 2003, Newcomb's most recent release is *Ride the High Country* (2008).

He lives in West Texas.

# JOHNNY NICHOLAS

### NOTHING LIKE A DON

This all started twenty-five years ago.

We had moved to the country to this little old gas station, beer joint, and roadhouse where my wife could cook. I had been on the road with my own bands and also with Asleep at the Wheel. When I left the Wheel, I had a band in Austin for a little while. But then I just decided to move to the country and paint my mailbox blue, as Taj Mahal said.

We had this little place. We sold gas and chili and gumbo. We hunted for our food and cut firewood for the wood stoves. It was pretty primitive, but it was good living. And I was playing for whoever wanted to listen.

One day, this guy, who was living way out in Melvin, Texas, walked in the door. He said, "I heard you played guitar and I've got an old Dobro I need to sell. I'm going to San Antonio and I need some money."

I said, "I'm not really into Dobros, but I'll take a look at it."

He brought in this guitar with a Dobro neck on it. I said, "That's not a Dobro. That's a National." I have a National. It's an old Style O that I bought in 1968. But that's another story.

I picked it up and played it. There was something about this guitar.

I was broke. I asked, "What do you want for it?"

He said he wanted seventy-five dollars.

It was a silver-bodied National. I think it was made in the '30s. I looked at it and said, "Here's this National guitar with a Dobro neck on it, and some asshole named Don inscribed his name on the bridge cover plate." Still, I took most of the money out of the cash register then went next door and robbed the piggy bank. I scraped together sixty-five dollars. I left about ten dollars in the register so if somebody came in, I could make change for beer or something.

I said, "Will you take sixty-five dollars?" He said he would.

I stuck it in the closet, but I found myself going back to it. I thought, "Man, I love the way this thing sounds." It just has this sweet sound.

But it also had issues. The resonator cone was compromised. And I wasn't crazy about the shape and feel of the Dobro neck. I like a meatier neck with a *V* on the back, like the old Nationals.

About a year later, Steve James came out and he brought Bob Brozman, who was a leading authority on National guitars.

They were in the dining room, having a bite to eat, and Steve said, "Hey, go get that National and show it to Bob."

I thought, "He doesn't want to see my old National with a Dobro neck and the cover plate that some asshole named Don carved his name on." I got the guitar out, but I was still thinking, "Bob Brozman does not want to see this piece of junk."

Brozman jumped out of his chair and took the guitar into the other room where there's more light. And he's studying this thing. Steve and I were scratching our heads, saying, "What the hell? What's he looking at?"

Brozman asked, "Where did you get this?"

I told him the story. Then I asked, "Why? What's the big deal?"

Brozman said, "Don't you know what this is?"

I said, "Yeah. It's an old National with a Dobro neck, and some asshole named Don carved his name in the bridge plate."

"No, this is the Don. This is the *Don*!"

The Don? What was this guy talking about?

He said, "I know that National made these, but I've never seen one."

It turns out this is a solid German silver body guitar. National made very few of them. I think maybe 150 total. Probably fewer

than that. Maybe 120. Anyway, it had the serial number on the end of the headstock. X88. So it was number 88 out of 120 guitars.

Brozman had all the old spec sheets from the old National factory. He worked closely with Don Young and all the guys who bought the National patents. They have built guitars for some time.

He told me to bring the guitar to San Luis Obispo, where the National factory is located. Brozman provided the spec sheets to Young so they could rebuild the guitar with the correct type of neck.

When I got it back, the neck was just like the one on my Style O, except it had a pearloid headstock. That neck cost four times what the guitar cost.

That's now my main axe for slide and finger-style guitar. I use two guitars on gigs, and I always carry the Don. It has a sound like nothing else.

Very few Dons had surfaced when Bob Brozman wrote his definitive book on Nationals five or six years after my encounter with him. My guitar is listed in there. It's an amazing book.

I've never seen another Don. I know they're out there. I talked to a vintage guitar dealer in Florida who has sold a couple of them. I know they all sound really good. There is something about the resonance and softness of the German silver that distinguishes that guitar from a brass-plated or a tin National. The cone is made from spun aluminum. It has beautiful hand-engraved herringbone borders on the body. It's a very simple and elegant guitar.

The National Style Os and the metal body National guitars are known for one sound, whereas the Don has a lot more depth, variety, and a wider range. A National is what it is and it gives you a great sound.

But there's nothing like a Don.

JOHNNY NICHOLAS has a love of blues and American roots music going back to a childhood surrounded by R&B, blues, country music, and rock music from the '50s and early '60s. After completing school, he crisscrossed the country, hopping freight trains, hitchhiking, and searching out the artists who had inspired him.

He has performed and recorded with such legends as Mississippi Fred McDowell, Bonnie Raitt, Snooky Pryor, Roosevelt Sykes, B. B. King, and Big Walter Horton. He has also played in and fronted many bands, including Guitar Johnny and the Rhythm Rockers, Asleep at the Wheel, Texas All-Stars, and Johnny Nicholas and Hellbent.

Nicholas tours internationally and plays regionally in Texas and South Louisiana. He made his recording debut as one of the featured artists on *Ann Arbor Blues & Jazz Festival 1972*. Since 1978, he has recorded six CDs under his own name.

Nicholas lives near Austin, Texas.

# JAMES PENNEBAKER

## CURTIS RAY'S LAP STEEL

I was touring with Lee Roy Parnell through most of the '90s, and I played pedal steel on a couple of songs in the show.

In 1997, we were at Billy Bob's Texas, a big nightclub in Fort Worth. A line of people were waiting to get Lee Roy's autograph after the show. He was doing a meet and greet.

I was walking out to the bus when a woman caught up to me. She told me that she was in Lee Roy's fan club. "I've been e-mailing him about an old Fender guitar that my mother has," she said. "It belonged to my brother. He died in 1955."

Immediately she had my attention because she was talking about a pre-1955 Fender guitar.

"What color is it?" I asked, and she told me that it was yellow. The earliest Telecasters were a butterscotch yellow. So, she really had my attention now.

She said she wanted to give it to Lee Roy because he plays slide.

I walked to the front of the line where he was busy signing autographs and told him about it. He said, "Yeah, I know what you're talking about. It's a lap steel. I'm not really interested."

So I went back to the woman, asked her a couple of questions, and verified that it was, in fact, a lap steel and not a Telecaster. I said that Lee Roy wasn't interested, but I might be interested in buying it.

She said her mother had taken it to some music stores around Dallas and was told it was worth about $250, which was about right for the time. She gave me her mother's phone number, and I called her when we got back to Nashville the next day.

She told me it had been in the attic for more than thirty years. They'd bought it for her son in the late '40s from McCord's Music in Dallas. McCord's was one of the first Fender dealers in the United States.

The boy's name was Curtis Ray Mitchell. He was born November 28, 1940, and he died February 17, 1955. All she told me was that he died in an electrical accident in the home.

She said the little buttons were gone, meaning that the tuning key buttons, which were made of celluloid, had just deteriorated. That's pretty common.

I told her I'd send a check for $250.

The next day I was thinking about it. If they bought a lap steel, they had to have an amplifier. You couldn't hear it without an amp. So I called her back. "Mrs. Mitchell, I'm just curious. When you bought the steel at McCord's, did you buy an amplifier with it?"

She said, "Yes, we did. If we have it, it would be in the garage. My son-in-law is coming over to pack that steel up so I'll have him look."

That afternoon she called back and said her son-in-law found the amplifier in the garage. She didn't know what kind of amp it was and it was already packed. She also wouldn't take any money for it because she said it went with the steel.

Over the next three or four days, I got out all my Fender books and found picture after picture of the Champion lap steel with the Champion 600 amp. And when I opened up the box, sure enough, it was a Champion 600 amp along with the steel that didn't have any buttons left.

I took it to Joe Glaser here in town. He's known all over the world for his repair skills. I told him that I needed to buy some replacement tuners.

"No, you don't," he said. "You don't need new tuners. You want to keep this thing original. You just need new buttons."

So I got new buttons on the tuners and it was as good as new. Everything was original. It never had a screw turned on it, and it's still that way.

That Christmas I got a card from the mother and the sister. Inside was a picture of this little boy sitting on the porch of a shotgun shack in his blue jeans, his Converse sneakers, and his T-shirt, and he's playing the lap steel plugged into the amp. On the back, it says "Curtis Ray Mitchell, born 11–28–40. Died 2–17–55."

We traded e-mails for a while. They were real happy, the mother especially, that the lap steel went to someone who appreciates it and uses it. And I have used both of them on records—the amplifier more than the steel. You plug a guitar into this amp, crank it, and stick a mic in front of it and you won't need any overdrive pedals or distortion pedals. You're there. It sounds huge.

When I bought the lap steel and amp, I promised I wouldn't resell it for money. I keep that picture in a frame next to the lap steel and amp in my studio.

So Curtis Ray is with his steel and amp. The three of them are still together.


The musical experience of JAMES PENNEBAKER began with a ¾-size violin. His classical training began in the third grade and continued into college.

His world changed when he saw the Beatles on *The Ed Sullivan Show*. He formed a country-rock band with high school friends. Despite being underage, they played clubs around Fort Worth.

He followed a 1976 tour with Delbert McClinton with stints in the house band at Dewey Groom's Longhorn Ballroom in Dallas and with Lee Mace's *Ozark Opry* in Missouri. In 1979, he rejoined McClinton, then took a break from touring in 1986 to perform and record.

Pennebaker has recorded and toured with Lee Roy Parnell, Pam Tillis, and others. Studio credits include producing and engineering two albums for Danny Flowers.

While still playing and recording, he is also the Nashville artist relations representative for Fishman Transducers, manufacturer of pickups for acoustic and electric guitars.

He lives in Nashville.

# LOUIE PÉREZ

My story is mostly about growing up in East Los Angeles. There was music in the house all the time. My mom loved ranchera singers—Miguel Aceves Mejía, Lola Beltrán, and Antonio Aguilar. When I was about eight years old, my dad died of a heart attack, and then there was a quiet period around the house. But the music came back, and I think that was kind of a salvation for my mom because it was something she had always loved.

She had this Bakelite radio on the kitchen counter and it was always playing Mexican music. When I got tall enough to reach the knobs, I discovered choice. I started listening to everything.

I had a plastic violin that I was always strumming. My mom saved her money and surprised me with an acoustic guitar from Milan's Music Store in East LA. It was a steel-string Stella. The strings were about three-quarters of an inch off the neck and it was painful to play. I didn't know what I was doing, but I played it and I loved it.

I met David Hidalgo in the tenth grade, and we connected over music. Time just evaporated as we listened to records and banged on guitars. When we started Los Lobos in 1973, the attraction for us was Mexican music. We had already been in bands. Conrad Lozano, who plays bass in Los Lobos, was in a band, and Cesar Rosas had been playing guitar in a Tower of Power-type band. So a lot of our friends who were musicians thought we were nuts to get into Mexican music. But we put aside the electric guitars and became completely immersed in it. Once we exhausted my mom's record collection and Cesar's mom's collection, we were in the record stores looking for this stuff. It was really unusual for young guys to embrace Mexican music because that was considered old people's music. With the whole homogenization thing, young people didn't want to listen to their parents' music.

The attraction wasn't purely cultural. It was more about the musicianship. We were listening to musicians we had no clue even existed and they played incredible guitar. When we put the needle on the record, we heard these guitarists playing Mexican regional music. And we were like, what the hell is that? And we thought Jimmy Page played fast!

We started looking for the instruments we'd seen on the covers of these records—like the *vihuela*, the *jarana*, and all these Mexican regional instruments. We'd go to pawnshops to buy them for ten or twenty bucks, and then we'd have no idea how to tune them or play them. We had to go around and ask other musicians for help.

I began playing the *jarana* when the band first started and I've been playing it ever since. My first *jarana* was a cheap one I found in 1973. The one I play now is an eight-string Mexican guitar. The stringed instruments are all guitar-based, but they change from region to region. We gravitated to the music of Veracruz.

When we made our way back to rock and roll in the late '70s, we needed a drummer. After being together for almost ten years, we weren't going to put out a classified ad. Dave is a really good drummer, but he played better accordion than I did, so I became the drummer, and until the mid-90s, I didn't play electric guitar in the band. My gig, at that point, was playing the folkloric Mexican instruments and then drums.

After almost twenty-five years, I made my way back to guitar, but the *jarana* has never let me down. I still play it in the band. I call my *jarana* Howard and he's my best friend. Howard's always got my back. If anything happened to my *jarana*, it would break my heart.

In 1988, when the band was celebrating our fifteenth anniversary, we had Candelas Guitars in Los Angeles build a matching *requinto* and *jarana*. The *requinto jarocho* is a four-string guitar that plays the melody and the *jarana* is the rhythm instrument. They go together; they're brothers. When we play regional Mexican music, Dave plays the *requinto*.

I pick up Howard whenever I feel like playing the *jarana*. I've got another *jarana* that was made by Manuel Delgado in Nashville. His name is Henry and I take him on the road. He's my workhorse. I don't want to say Howard is retired because as soon as I start strumming, he comes alive. He says, "Where ya been?" He speaks to me in Spanish. When he speaks in English, it's a little broken. He's got a heavy accent.

Dave and I wrote "La Pistola y El Corazón" on Howard. It's on the album by the same name, and we won a Grammy for that album in 1988. And the song "Be Still" on *The Neighborhood* album is all Howard. That was the first time we wrote a song that was sung in English, but the music is influenced by traditional Mexican music.

If I were just going to be a *jarana* player, I'd be happy being just that. It's something I've always gone back to.

Multi-instrumentalist and songwriter LOUIE PÉREZ is a founding member of the multiple Grammy Award-winning Los Lobos. His work has been featured on every Los Lobos album since *And a Time to Dance* (1983). Pérez and bandmate David Hidalgo have also written songs for their critically acclaimed side project, the Latin Playboys.

His songs have been covered by Robert Plant, Waylon Jennings, and Jerry Garcia, among others. He has written songs for an adaptation of Bertolt Brecht's *The Good Person of Szechwan*, and he co-wrote the book for the play *Evangeline, the Queen of Make Believe*.

His prose has appeared in the *Los Angeles Times Magazine*, *LA Weekly*, and *BOMB*, a New York arts journal.

Pérez handled editorial direction and art supervision for *El Cancionero: Más y Más*, which was nominated for a Grammy for Best Boxed Recording Package in 2001.

He lives in Southern California.

# CASPER RAWLS

## CONNECTED UP, AUSTIN STYLE

I have a '68 Paisley Telecaster that was originally owned by Steven Hennig. He's the son of Ray Hennig, who owned the famous Austin music store, Heart of Texas Music.

Steven shipped the Telecaster to Gene Parsons in California to install a B-Bender on it. That's a custom, handmade device that stretches the B string. That stretching gives the guitar a sound similar to a steel guitar.

Steven is a great guitar player, just amazing. But he got the B-Bender back and he hated it. He couldn't use it. He didn't like it. He didn't need it. He plays that stuff with his hands.

So he traded it off to another famous Austin guitar player who has since passed away, Danny Thorpe. Danny played guitar for Billy Joe Shaver and many other groups in Austin over the years. He didn't like the B-Bender either. So he put a Bigsby Palm Pedal on it and that acts as a vibrato. It moves all the strings.

That Telecaster eventually passed through a bunch of hands and ended up with some guys in Oklahoma. They removed the B-Bender and the Bigsby Palm Pedal and put a bunch of Eddie Van Halen pickups in it.

Eventually they sold it to Jay Hudson in Austin. Jay had a studio called the Hit Shack. Somehow, I got word that Jay had that guitar and I begged and begged him to sell it to me. He finally agreed.

I put the B-Bender back in it. I called my friend Seymour Duncan who makes guitar pickups. I wanted different pickups, and I knew

exactly what I wanted them to sound like. I told Seymour I wanted a pickup that sounds like James Burton and Don Rich put together.

When I got the guitar back, I plugged it in and it was perfect. It was my sound. I called him and said, "Seymour, remember what you did on this pickup."

He said, "I know exactly what I did and we're going to call it the Casper model from now on. When you call for a pickup, just ask for your model."

By that time, I was in a band called the LeRoi Brothers, based in Austin. I joined them in 1985 and that Tele became my main guitar. I took it all over the world. When we were in San Francisco, I was at a place called Stars Guitars. I saw a bridge I liked and I bought it. It was perfect.

Ray Flacke, a brilliant British guitarist who played with Ricky Skaggs for many years, was giving a clinic in a Dallas music store, and while I was waiting for him to begin, I noticed a bunch of

Fender guitar necks hanging on the wall. I picked one up and, lo and behold, I found the perfect neck. I replaced the original neck with the new one. My guitar was complete. This was what I wanted.

James Burton came through Austin with Elvis Costello. My friend, Dan Forte, was kind enough to take my pick guard to James and he autographed it. It's about worn off because the guitar has been around the world, but you can see a faint remnant of his autograph. I have a pick James used and I put it under the pick guard. It's a clear pick guard so you can see his pick.

Since then, I've been so blessed to know James as a friend. When he was inducted into the Shreveport Hall of Fame, I was there. He had all his guitars laid out and I had brought mine . . . and so we swapped. He let me play his paisley and he played mine.

James Burton's Telecaster was one of the best Telecasters, if not the best Telecaster, I've played in my life. But James wasn't too hip on mine. He said, "This guitar needs some work. We've got to get this to Seymour."

It's a total mongrel of different parts, but it is totally me and everything I ever wanted that guitar to be. It's all connected up Austin-style. It's perfect.

Bitten by the music bug as a boy in Helotes, Texas, CASPER RAWLS regularly rode his bicycle to John T. Floore's Country Store to catch country music acts.

He developed his own sound by studying the work of James Burton and Don Rich and incorporating the B-string bender. Playing in a succession of bands while attending the University of Texas in the early 1970s, he also worked as a sound tech and rigger for major bands like Styx, Heart, and Supertramp.

He's put in twenty-five years playing with the LeRoi Brothers, nine with Toni Price, five with Doyle Bramhall, and two with Kelly Willis. He has played on dozens of recording sessions. His debut album, *Brave World*, was released in 2015.

Rawls plays regularly throughout central Texas.

He lives in Helotes.

# G. E. SMITH

## A GOOD GUITAR IS A GOOD GUITAR

In the mid-'70s, I was living in this little Connecticut town called Yalesville. There was a guy up in Hartford, Steve Kubicka, who would get stuff, and I would visit with him sometimes. One time he had a 1960 Les Paul Custom with three pickups. Almost all the parts you could take off the guitar were in a grocery bag. The husk of the guitar was just leaning in the corner. It was one of the most worn Les Pauls I'd ever seen, but it was not broken.

I asked him about it and he said, "Well, I just got it. The pickups are supposed to not work. And I don't know how to wire the three pickups with the toggle switch."

I don't remember what I had that he wanted. It was either a Gibson acoustic or a Les Paul Goldtop—something that had cost me less than a hundred dollars. So I offered my guitar for the Les Paul Custom.

He agreed because this Les Paul Custom didn't seem like any big deal. Hundred-buck stuff.

I gradually put it back together. The hardest part was figuring out how to wire a Custom, but eventually, a buddy and I got it going.

Two of the pickups are original. The neck pickup is one of the best humbuckers I've ever heard. The bridge pickup was broken, and back then, there wasn't anybody who re-wrapped pickups. But I knew guys who had parts and sold things. For $150, I bought a 1959 zebra pickup; the kind with one white coil and one black coil. The cover had never been off of it. That pickup now would be worth thousands.

It does all the Les Paul stuff. A good sustain can sound real clean, but the really great ones have a certain kind of harmonic depth. It's a combination of really great pickups and the wood . . . everything. Everything counts on a guitar. It has a couple of the best PAF pickups I've ever heard.

This one must be from early 1960 because it still had some meat on the neck. The later 1960 necks got really skinny. I like a neck that is the same depth at the first fret as it is at the twelfth. A lot of the resonance—particularly on an acoustic—comes from the neck as much as from the body. A guitar with a really skinny neck will have a different vibration, a brighter, more trebly sound. Some guys love that. But I like it fat and growly.

The strap was tossed on stage by a fan. I think it was in Boston. I picked it up and read the message she wrote in pen. *To G. E. with lots love Kris.* She included her phone number.

Originally, the parts were all gold. Now the gold is completely worn off except for a little left on the tuners. Somebody played it a ton. Then I put a lot more wear on it.

This stuff got to be crazy valuable in the '90s. Collectors really drove the prices up. Before eBay, you could still find stuff, but now you can't find anything anywhere. Now most of the great guitars are put away.

This is what I don't understand. Guitars are tools. Would a carpenter get a hammer, use it a few times, and say, "Wow! This is the best hammer I've ever owned." Then put it away and not use it? No, he wouldn't.

I used to be a real vintage snob. The guitar had to be all original, a certain year, this, that. But more and more, I think a good guitar is a good guitar. I don't care who made it or when or where. If somebody's playing it and they like to play it, that's all that matters.

There's a reason I've kept the Custom. I've used it extensively since I traded for it. I've used it on several number one recordings and tons of records. If someone calls me for a job and they know my playing and have heard it, they'll ask me to use the Custom.

I've had a lot of guitars over the years that I've sold, but there are a few that stayed. There was never any question about selling the Custom. It's magic. It's just a killer. It stays.

G. E. SMITH got his hands on a guitar when he was seven years old. As a teenager, he played in bars around his native Pennsylvania. In the 1970s, he toured with the Scratch Band, and by 1979, he was playing lead guitar with Hall & Oates, constantly touring, recording, and playing on their biggest hits.

Ten years of leading the *Saturday Night Live* band resulted in an Emmy award and a Grammy-nominated album collaboration with Buddy Guy. Then came four years playing lead guitar in Bob Dylan's band, and since 2010, Smith has played on Roger Waters's The Wall Live tour.

Over the years, he has been tapped for musical director of several high-profile events, including the 1988 Emmy Awards, the Rock and Roll Hall of Fame concert, and Bob Dylan's 30th Anniversary Concert.

Smith lives on Long Island.

# JD SOUTHER

I'd like to tell you a story about a guitar that went a long way in a very short time.

It was 1976, and I was the special guest on the Eagles' Hotel California tour. When we played Houston, we met a guy named Tony Dukes, who sold guitars. He tried to match particular instruments to individual musicians. He came to our show with a Les Paul for Joe Walsh, another guitar for Don Felder, and a Gibson Everly Brothers model for me.

The Everly Brothers model was in great shape, absolutely beautiful. It had one tiny mark on the lower shoulder of the guitar where it had rested on a previous owner's leg when he played. "Oh, my God!" I said when he opened the case. I strummed the opening chords for "The Last in Love." I said, "Yeah, this is it."

I had actually been talking for several months about wanting a really good, old Everly Brothers model guitar. It's basically a fancier version of the J-185, with double pick guards and stars on the neck instead of dots.

That guitar cost a considerable amount of money, but I loved it. It was exactly what I was looking for. Dukes obviously knew what artists liked in their instruments—I think everything he brought that night was purchased by someone.

Not long after that, it was stolen, along with another guitar of mine—I think it was a Gibson J-45. We never really knew for sure if the guitars were stolen on the road or when things were packed

up to go home or after they got back to LA to my cartage company. It had been back to California in the studio and then back out on the road with me. I'm thinking it was stolen somewhere in the Northeast.

At any rate, my favorite guitar was gone.

When I still had the guitar, Jimmy Buffett saw it a couple of times and said he would love to have one like it. About a year after the theft, I was at his house in Aspen. After dinner, he said, "Drac, I got one just like yours." That's his nickname for me. Dracula.

"One what?" I asked.

With kind of a twinkle in his eye, he brought this guitar out. "Look," he said, "a '59 Everly Brothers."

There was that one tiny flaw on the surface. "That's my guitar," I said.

Jimmy turned white. I gave him the serial number because I still had it in my head. It was a pretty fresh wound.

He looked inside the guitar, and there it was.

I said again, "That's my guitar." The room got very quiet.

There was no question about it. It was even the same case.

Jimmy said, "Oh man, what am I gonna do?"

His wife, Jane, said, "Well, what you're gonna do is give John David his guitar back."

"You're right," he said. "You're absolutely right."

I said, "God bless ya, Bubba. It's the right thing to do." That's my nickname for him. Bubba.

Jimmy and I talked about whether to go after the Florida dealer who sold him the guitar, but we decided not to.

The other guitar was never recovered. Jimmy said he never saw it, so presumably it was sold before he got there.

I'm just fascinated that this one guitar covered so much ground in a year—from Houston to California to the Northeast to Florida—and managed to find its way back to me at a friend's house in Aspen. I think it's a fairly phenomenal journey.

I wrote half the stuff on the *You're Only Lonely* album with that guitar. I wrote "White Rhythm and Blues" on that guitar. I wrote the song that the Dixie Chicks cut, "I'll Take Care of You" on that guitar. That was my go-to guitar on stage for many years. And I still use it in the studio and on stage.

Later I think Jimmy got another one just like it.

JD SOUTHER is a songwriter and performer associated with the 1970s country-rock sound of Southern California.

Souther co-wrote several hits with the Eagles—including "Heartache Tonight," "Victim of Love," and "Best of My Love"—and has written for or co-written with artists such as Linda Ronstadt, Jimmy Buffett, Dixie Chicks, Joe Cocker, George Strait, and many others. He has released eight solo albums and two albums as a member of the Souther/Hillman/Furay Band. His most recent album, *Tenderness*, was released in 2015.

He has had acting roles in the television shows *Thirtysomething* and *Nashville* and the 1990 film *Postcards From the Edge*.

He lives in Nashville.

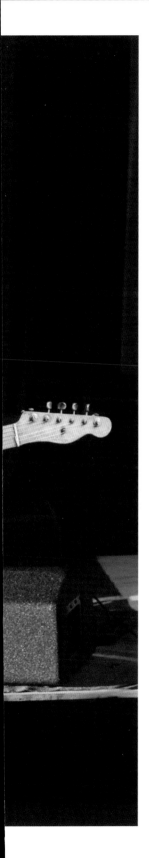

# MARTY STUART

## CLARENCE WHITE'S '54 TELE

Clarence White's 1954 Telecaster is a guitar that I never dreamed I would own. But, from the day I got it, it became a lifelong exploration into the proper art of string bending.

In 1972, Clarence's brother, Roland, who played with Lester Flatt's band, invited me to ride along on the band's bus. This was Labor Day weekend. Lester heard Roland and me playing in the back, and he said, "Y'all do that on stage this weekend." So we did. The crowd liked it, and at the end of the weekend, Lester offered me a job. I was thirteen years old.

The first place I lived in Nashville was Roland's house. I could not have asked for a better place to stay. Roland is such a world-class musical citizen. We played music constantly: the Grand Ole Opry, concerts, jam sessions, recording sessions, radio shows, and television shows. Our instruments seldom cooled off.

Roland also had a great record collection, and he made me feel perfectly welcome to use it. One particular record that caught my eye was by the Kentucky Colonels, a band that he and Clarence had back in California. The album was titled *Appalachian Swing*. That was the record that introduced me to Clarence's style of acoustic guitar playing. Another one of my favorite discoveries in Roland's collection was a recording called *Untitled* by the Byrds. It was a double-record set with the first disc being studio and the second disc being a live recording of a Byrds concert. The live side was spellbinding.

That was the record that introduced me to Clarence's electric guitar playing. I'd never heard playing like that. It was part steel guitar. It was rock and roll, it was country, and it was bluegrass. Clarence's playing was astoundingly innovative, pure genius. He played from a stratosphere all his own. I remember having the feeling of knowing that even as great as he was, he was just scratching the surface. It's unimaginable where he would have taken the guitar by now.

All those possibilities were silenced when he died in 1973. A few years later, his wife, Susie, moved from California to her home state of Kentucky. I first met Susie at Roland's house when she and her children came to Nashville to visit. Susie, Bradley, and Michelle became like family to me.

Susie called me one night in early 1980. "I need to sell some guitars and some other things," she said. I knew she was serious, so a couple of days later, I made arrangements and drove from Nashville to Elkhorn City, Kentucky.

One of the guitars that she was ready to let go of was a 1954 Stratocaster. It had been used as a parts guitar for Clarence's Tele. I played it and then I asked, "Is the Telecaster here?" I just wanted to look at it.

She laughed, "I knew that's what you really wanted to see."

What makes this particular Telecaster so special, beyond being owned and played by Clarence, is that this guitar is the first string bender—or pull string, as it is now famously known. The pull string is a mechanism attached to the strap that allows you to bend the B string up to a C-sharp, giving the guitar the sound of a pedal steel. Clarence and Gene Parsons were the masterminds behind the guitar, but Gene was really the architect.

Susie showed me to the guitar. It was in the attic of her house in a blue-and-white road case that had "Byrds" stenciled on it. She opened it up and there it was. I picked it up. I couldn't believe I was holding it. I had no idea how to play it.

Susie said, "That's the one you want, isn't it?" I didn't even have an answer.

She suggested that I buy the Stratocaster, the Telecaster, one of Clarence's Nudie suits, and some Byrds paraphernalia.

I had just gone to work for Johnny Cash and had saved a little money. I laid my checkbook down on the table and said, "Put whatever number you need within reason. If I don't have it, I'll go borrow it."

She wrote, "$1,450."

I said, "Susie, the E string on that guitar is worth a thousand dollars."

"I know what the guitar is worth," she said. "This is exactly how much I want. This is exactly how much I need."

She wrote out a bill of sale on a piece of notebook paper for $1,450.

I took the Telecaster home to Nashville. The first gig it ever worked was a *Saturday Night Live* performance that I played with Cash.

The only things I've changed on Clarence's guitar are I moved one of the Scruggs tuner from the fifth string to the sixth string, and I had Ralph Mooney put a palm pedal on it, which lowers the

E string by a half-step. Beyond that, the dirt on it is the same as the day I got it. To my ears, it's the perfect Tele, and I don't want to mess with its mojo.

After getting the guitar, I felt unworthy to have it because I didn't know how to play it and do right by it. I'm sure there were a lot of guitar players who were much more qualified than me to have that Tele, but I took it seriously and worked hard on learning to play it. Back then, I didn't have to worry about being up front and center on stage. I always had a singer in front of me and I could stand back, explore, and experiment and try and figure things out. I played it on a lot of Cash records, and then I started making my own records in the late '80s, had a bunch of hits, and it was on most of them.

The most fun I've ever had with it is when the Fabulous Superlatives and I did some shows with Roger McGuinn. We got to be the Byrds. Roger was out front. I just stood behind him and played

Clarence's parts to the best of my ability. I loved hearing Roger's Rickenbacker twelve-string and Clarence's Tele back together, making music again. It was magical.

In 2010, I wrote a song called "Hummingbyrd" and dedicated it to Clarence. I recorded it with the Fabulous Superlatives at the historic RCA Studio B in Nashville. The song won a Grammy. It made me feel a little vindicated for having the guitar.

Perhaps it's self-imposed, but I believe there's a responsibility that comes with owning that guitar. I respect its legacy, but legacy will carry you only so far. The most important thing you can do with a guitar like that is to continue to make new music and new history with it. That's what keeps the story moving forward—as it should.

MARTY STUART began his career at age twelve, performing with the Sullivan Family Bluegrass Gospel Singers. At thirteen, he was invited by Lester Flatt to join his band. He later played in recording sessions before joining Johnny Cash's band in 1980 and then launching a solo career in 1985.

With his band, the Fabulous Superlatives, he blends traditional country, bluegrass, and gospel with honky-tonk. He has more than twenty albums and five Grammy Awards to his credit. A member of the Grand Ole Opry, he has served as president of the Country Music Foundation. He has also published three volumes of photographs, showcasing portraits of country music artists.

He lives in Nashville with his wife, country singer Connie Smith.

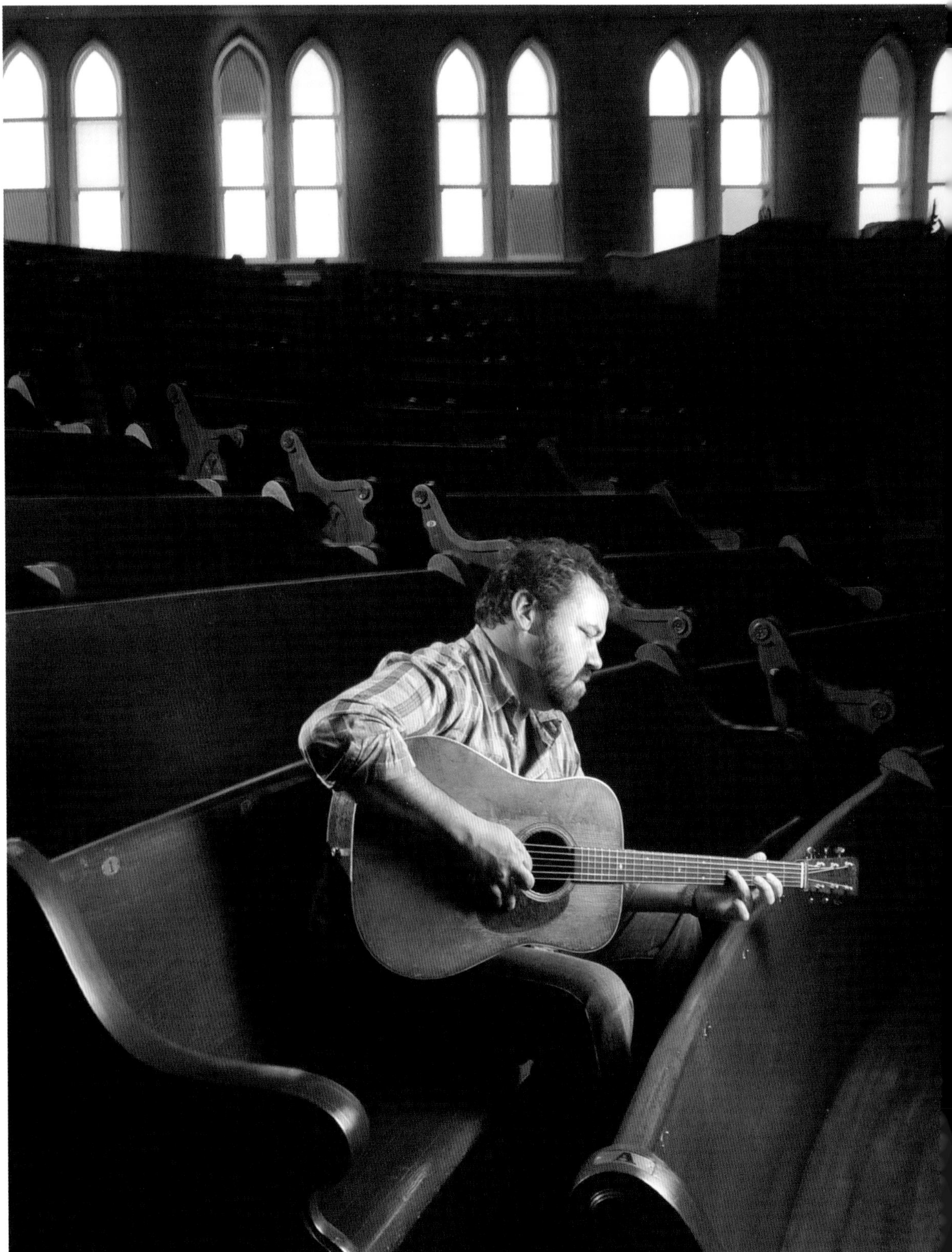

# DAN TYMINSKI

I've been with Alison Krauss and Union Station for twenty years, but when I joined the band, I was not a guitar player. I had never even owned a guitar. I joined under the pretense that I would get a guitar and sit in the closet until I had it figured out. For the first couple of months, I borrowed a guitar from my bandmate, Ron Block. And I put the word out that I was looking for an instrument.

At the Bass Mountain Bluegrass Festival in North Carolina, a man came up to me and said, "Hey, are you the guy looking for a guitar?" I said I was and asked him what he had. He looked over his shoulder and very quietly said, "I think it's a Martin."

All bluegrass guys pretty much play Martins. That wasn't enough information to spike my interest, so I hopped in my van and headed to the gate. A different man came running up and said, "Hey, are you Dan? I understand you're looking for a guitar."

I asked, "What is it?"

He said, "It's one that you'll want to see." That was what I needed to hear. I was looking for something special.

I picked it up and hit a couple of strings and it was instant love. I thought I was the luckiest man in the world. I played a few chords and then I noticed the herringbone binding. I was playing a 1946 herringbone D-28. That was the last year Martin made what they call the pre-war herringbones, which they started making in 1934. It's the staple of what bluegrass guys play.

I said, "I really appreciate your time, but this is way out of my price range."

He said, "You might be surprised."

As it turned out, it had some cracks that had been fixed, so it wasn't full retail price. Still, I ended up borrowing money from a friend and then from the bank to buy the guitar. I paid on it like a house for three years.

I remember the week I paid the guitar off. We were getting ready to go on stage and I announced, "Boys, she's all mine!" And as I said that, the strap came loose and the guitar hit the ground. The G string tuner was bent in such a way that I couldn't change the string. What was on my mind through that whole show was if I break the string, I can't finish the show because I had no backup guitar. This was my one and only. It was a nervous show, but we made it through.

Since then, I've had a few other Martins—a '34 herringbone, a '37, and a '42. But I measure everything against my first guitar. It is still the best guitar I've played for the tonal qualities. It can play very soft and pretty, but it's also probably the most aggressive, snarly-toothed guitar for the heavy-handed stuff that I like to do. And it marries well with other instruments. It has its own place in any band setting. I've used it to record with dozens of other bands and there's no struggle to make it heard. You don't have to brighten it or darken it.

I got the most back-handed compliment from a luthier when I handed him my guitar. He played a couple of chords, handed it back to me, and said, "Wow! You're a lot better than I thought you were." I thought, "Thank you?"

He said that because my action is really high. I like a high action and I play hard. I've always played hard. I grew up a banjo player and I've always had a high action on my banjos. People hated my banjo and they struggle with my guitar.

Right after I bought it, I was on the bus playing it and our bass player asked who Dorcey Lewis was. I looked at him with a blank expression and said, "I have no idea."

"Well, his name is on your guitar," he said.

Someone had glued mailbox letters on the front of the guitar. To this day, if the light is just so and if the angle is right and if the stars are in line, you can see the name "Dorcey Lewis."

I talked to the guy I bought it from and mentioned the name. He looked at me like, "How would you know that name?" He hadn't noticed it either. He told me Dorcey Lewis was an old man who had previously owned the guitar and had played it around town for years.

I think this guitar has been prepared for me since it was made in 1946. It was meant to be mine. People spend lifetimes searching for their perfect instrument, their Holy Grail. I was looking for a guitar, but the guitar found me. I tried to drive away from it. A guy ran me down and I tried to drive away again.

It was my first guitar and it will be my last.

DAN TYMINSKI, a fourteen-time Grammy Award winner, is a bluegrass guitarist, mandolin player, and vocalist.

After starting out in high school as a banjo player, the Vermont native played mandolin in the Lonesome River Band before joining Alison Krauss and Union Station. Tyminski has been named Vocalist of the Year four times by the International Bluegrass Music Association.

Tyminski provided the singing voice for the George Clooney character in the film, *O Brother, Where Art Thou?* His vocals helped "I Am a Man of Constant Sorrow," a single from the soundtrack, become the Country Music Association Single of the Year and win a Grammy Award for Country Collaboration with Vocals.

His solo albums include *Carry Me Across the Mountain* (2000) and *Wheels* (2008).

Tyminski lives in Nashville.

# REDD VOLKAERT

## THAT GOOD BUCK OWENS SOUND

This one particular guitar I got when I was thirteen years old. It's a Fender Esquire. It's like a Telecaster, but it has only one pickup back by the bridge. Telecaster has that as well, but also one close to the neck.

The factory didn't put that neck pickup in these Esquire guitars, and they didn't cut the hole in the pick guard. But the hole's in the body because it's the identical guitar. They just left one pickup out, knocked sixty bucks off the price, and called it a "student line guitar."

When I was a kid, I had two paper routes. I wanted to start buying guitars. Back then, I was making pretty good money for a little guy. I think I made sixty dollars a month.

My dad played pool a lot and kinda made his living doing that for a while. He played snooker with a buddy who owned a music store. One day, my dad comes home with this guitar. He had beaten his buddy in a snooker tournament. This particular day, this guy didn't have any money, so he said, "Hey, you can take it out in guitars."

So Dad got this Esquire. The guitar was a '58 and this was maybe 1972. It was an older guitar, but it was like new. Whoever bought it probably took a few lessons, got sore fingers, quit, and put it under the bed. So when they brought it to the music store to sell, all it had was a coffee stain on the case. The lacquer hadn't even been rubbed off the metal frets on the neck.

Dad said, "I got this guitar in a pool game. It's from Hoffman's Music and it's got that really good Buck Owens sound. I think you're gonna like it."

I picked it up and played it. It was really, really clean. It even smelled new. I was jacked about that guitar.

Then he said, "I'll sell it to you. It's gonna be two hundred dollars, and you can pay me from your paper route money. You can play it on Sundays for about twenty minutes until it's paid for."

I was thinking, "What good's that? I can't play it?"

Of course, he was trying to teach me the value of the dollar, about making payments and waiting my turn until it was paid for, and about the respect of that.

"Well, can I take it to school and show some guys?"

"No, it don't leave the house at all," he said. "You can look at it on Sundays or have them come over to look at it, but it ain't paid for. So it's still mine."

I paid the thing off, started playing it, and fell in love with it.

And it wasn't a year or so later that I noticed these guys who were playing in bands had Telecasters with two pickups. I thought "Man, I'm missing out. I've gotta get another pickup for this thing."

So I went over to the music store and they gave me this Gibson pickup. It was an old one out of a Les Paul, so it was a lot bigger than what would have gone in at the Fender factory. I'm fourteen years old at this point, so, of course, I'm thinking, "I can get it in there."

I took the pick guard off. I got a screwdriver and a hammer and cut a big hole to house that pickup. I took a pocket knife, heated it up, and cut the hole in the pick guard to fit the pickup. It was just a tad sloppy.

I've since cleaned the hole up with a router because I was so embarrassed about how bad it looked. Not that anyone could see it under the guard, but it mattered to me.

I still have that Esquire, and it's just a great guitar. It's seen a million gigs and hotel rooms and the backs of pickup trucks.

Playing-wise, it feels better every year because it wears just right. I'm used to every little nick and groove. The neck's got some wear on it, but the indentations feel like the shape of my fingers.

It's not the same guitar that I got when I was a kid. I could not replace that guitar even with the price of a vintage, mint condition '58 Esquire. It's been through all kinds of hell. Just like an old shoe, every little dent and groove in it is mine.

REDD VOLKAERT is best known for playing guitar in Merle Haggard's band, the Strangers.

A native of British Columbia, Volkaert moved to the United States in 1986, playing in different bands and clubs in California. He moved to Nashville in 1990, sitting in at clubs and substituting for other players. He established himself first with the Don Kelly Band and later with Clinton Gregory.

Now in Austin, Volkaert plays in two bands—The Redd Volkaert Band and HeyBale—that have played weekly for fifteen years at the Continental Club.

He has recorded with Haggard, Brad Paisley, Cindy Cashdollar and Dale Watson, among others. With James Burton, Vince Gill, Albert Lee, Brent Mason and Steve Wariner, Volkaert played on Paisley's 2008 song, "Cluster Pluck," which won the Grammy for Best Country Instrumental Performance.

He lives in Cedar Creek, Texas.

# WADDY WACHTEL

## THE BEST DEAL EVER

I moved to Los Angeles in the summer of 1968 with a band that never really got off the ground. Looking back, I think that was probably just as well.

Within a few days of moving there, I met David Crosby. Not long after that, he introduced me to Stephen Stills. They were about to form Crosby, Stills & Nash. It was an amazing time to be in LA.

Our band was soon sharing rehearsal rooms with CSN. Although Neil Young was not officially in their band, he was there a lot.

Stills and Young had filled the walls of that room with guitars. There must have been fifty guitars there, and a lot of them were Les Pauls.

At the time, I was playing a beautiful Gibson Super 400, but what I really wanted was another Les Paul. I had had what they call a Les Paul Jr. for many years, but I sold it to my prize student, Leslie West, before I moved to the West Coast.

I asked Stephen if he would sell one of his Les Pauls. "Let's trade rehearsal rooms tonight," he said, "and you pick the one you want."

I spent the night in that room and came out with a 1960 Sunburst Les Paul. I gave Stephen $350 for it, and that was the best deal ever. Of all the Les Pauls I played, it had the brightest sound. It's one of the most valuable, most coveted guitars. I broke the neck on mine so many times that it had to be replaced, but even with the replacement neck, it's still very valuable.

To me, most Les Pauls feel like a baseball bat. They have a very thick neck. But the neck on my 1960 Les Paul is shaved down. The fret board on top is like glass. You can move like crazy all over it. It's very narrow from the back of the neck to the fret board. The 1960 models are the only ones with necks like that. I don't know if they are all like that, but mine is. It's perfect for me.

That was my go-to guitar. It's played on more hit records than any other guitar I've used. I used it on "It's So Easy" by Linda Ronstadt and on "Edge of Seventeen" by Stevie Nicks. It's the one on "Oh Sherrie" by Steve Perry. Anything you hear on Warren Zevon's records is that Les Paul. I took it on the road with the Everly Brothers, Carole King, James Taylor, Linda Ronstadt, and Keith Richards.

One night I was playing my gig at The Joint in Los Angeles and the neck started going out. So I decided I had to retire it. Now I only record with it at home. I use it on movie tracks or if someone sends me a track to record on at home. But if it leaves the house, the insurance is cancelled.

Years ago, I was in the studio with Keith Richards. He picks up my Les Paul and starts playing it. He says, "Hey Wads, now I see why you always drag this fuckin' thing around. This guitar is incredible. It has the best neck."

If you remember when the Stones were on *Ed Sullivan*, Keith was playing a sunburst Les Paul with a Bigsby on it. So I'm looking at him holding my Les Paul, and I said, "Keith, what happened to your sunburst Les Paul?"

"I have no idea," he said.

"Wouldn't it be funny," I asked, "if somehow Steve Stills wound up getting yours and I bought it from him and that guitar you're playing turned out to be your original sunburst Les Paul?"

We were never able to trace it back to Keith because Stephen could not remember where he got it. Who knows? It could be the same one.

New York native **WADDY WACHTEL** ranks among the most successful session players in rock music with an impressive resumé that spans a five-decade career.

His studio credits include work with Keith Richards, the Rolling Stones, Linda Ronstadt, Jackson Browne, Warren Zevon, Stevie Nicks, Bonnie Raitt, Randy Newman, Ronnie Wood, Bryan Ferry, Ringo Starr, Neil Young, Joe Walsh, and James Taylor.

Wachtel has played on concert tours with the Everly Brothers, Stevie Nicks, James Taylor, Linda Rondstadt, and Keith Richards's band the X-Pensive Winos, among others.

His numerous film work includes playing guitar and composing original music for the Jimi Hendrix movie, *Jimi: All Is by My Side*.

Wachtel lives in Los Angeles.

# DUSTIN WELCH

## A CATALOG GUITAR

I had been noodling around on my dad's guitars when he said, "Should we get you an instrument?" My dad's guitar player had a neighbor, Kent Blazy, who wrote some hits for Garth Brooks. Kent was getting rid of instruments, and Dad gave him about three hundred dollars for a Carson J. Robison. I was eight years old when we bought that weird old Wards catalog guitar.

Dad would read bedtime stories to us. When I got this guitar, I'd make him teach me a new song every night instead. Then the next day, I'd work on it, and after dinner, I'd say, "Okay, what's next?"

I have a lot of memories of studying and learning with this guitar. I went to some after-school guitar classes. Everybody else there had newer Epiphones or Seagulls, and then I'd come walking in with this ancient catalog guitar. I always loved that kind of stuff.

When I was ten, I carved a design in it. My mom's family is Osage Indian, and there's a particular spider design that they tattoo on their hands. Native Americans think of the spider as a symbol of creativity. According to Osage legend, a chief went out in the woods, looking for different animals. He had his head down, following deer tracks, and he ran into a big spider web. The spider asked the chief what he was doing down there, and he told the spider he was looking for animals that he could name his clans after. The spider asked, "Why don't you name one after me?" The chief told him that he was just an insignificant spider.

"Yes," the spider replied, "But I'm patient."

And that's true. The spider spins his web and he just waits. Patience and creativity are two things the spider symbolizes, and I identify with that. So I carved the design on the front of the guitar on the shoulder. At first, it ticked my dad off. But later he said, "Actually, that's really cool."

A couple of years later, I needed a pickup. There was an old Sunrise pickup at my dad's house and I asked him if I could put it in. It turns out it was given to him by Howie Epstein, who played bass with Tom Petty and the Heartbreakers.

I still use that pickup. It was duct-taped just inside the sound hole. I finally got that changed, but for a long time, it was an identifying feature of this guitar. I'd show up at gigs and I'd have to find some new duct tape. There are other pickups I could try, but I'm sentimental about this Sunrise.

I played this guitar in my high school bands and all my subsequent bands. For a while, I was mostly playing banjo and resonator guitar, so it wasn't touring with me. But it was still my primary instrument. All the songs I've written started on this thing.

Without being plugged in, it's great in the studio. My dad even recorded a track with it years ago. The song was called "Beneath My Wheels." He had it tuned down to a B. It was about as low as you could get it without the strings flapping around. He probably used medium strings.

It's an odd instrument. It's a little cranky. The tuners squeak, and I break at least a couple of strings at every gig. It's not easy to play for a lot of folks. The neck is fatter and the action is pretty difficult. But it feels natural to me. It's so unique that it has really defined my way of playing. Having to work a little harder on that instrument made me develop a certain style. Maybe I play it more aggressively because of that, but it can take a beating. I've all but destroyed it.

I was lucky to have a cool guitar like that to learn on. I'm now thirty-two years old and I've been playing this guitar for twenty-four years. My hands basically grew up around the neck of this thing.

Raised in a creative environment in Nashville, DUSTIN WELCH began playing music at an early age. Playing in bands led him to songwriting.

The multi-instrumentalist is as comfortable playing folk and roots music as he is blasting out rock and roll, including playing with the Celtic punk band the Scotch Greens.

His songs have been recorded by Louise Goffin, John Fulbright, and Justin Townes Earle, among others, and he has played on the sessions of other artists.

Welch also founded Soldier Songs and Voices, a national organization providing veterans free instruments and instruction in music and songwriting.

He lives in Austin.

# KEVIN WELCH

## LITTLE SISTER

I'm pretty close with all my guitars. I'm not a guy who has ever had very many guitars. I know a lot of people who buy and sell them all the time and more power to 'em. They're into it and they enjoy that stuff, but I would feel awful if I sold one of my guitars.

I've got a little Martin 00-18 that was made in 1959. It was my first good acoustic guitar, and I've played it on just about everything I've ever recorded. Guitars have personalities, and that's why I think every guitar deserves a name. Mine's called "Little Sister." My friend Mike Henderson is the one who named her that and it just stuck.

I got this guitar from a friend of mine, Jack Long, back in about 1973 or 1974. Jack had bought it from a fiddle player named Glenn Godsey. Right after I got it, I happened to meet Glenn Godsey one evening in a bar in Tulsa. I was pretty excited about meeting him because he was sort of a famous guy around there. I said, "Mr. Godsey, I ended up with that 00-18 Martin that you sold to Jack Long."

He looked at me really, really hard, and then he turned around and stormed off. He wouldn't even talk to me. It was like he was pissed off that he had sold it. That was the last time I ever saw the guy.

I took it to my parents' house to show them. I sat down and put the guitar in my lap. My dad's bird dog walked over and looked at me. And in this lightning fast move, he put his paw up and scratched the guitar from top to the bottom. That hurt. But now I've had the thing so long that the scratch has faded.

When I got Little Sister, I was a young, dumbass guitar player. I remember thinking that the tuners looked bad. So I decided that they must be getting ready to go, and I ordered some gold Schaller or Grover mini tuners that were popular at the time. Thank God, those things never came in and I never did change them. To this day, they are exactly as bad as they were the day I got that guitar, and I've never had any trouble with them.

I was making a record one time with Don Was and Tony Brown producing. It was a Kelly Willis record. The other acoustic guitar player on the session was Billy Bremner, this great guitarist who'd been in Rockpile.

Don's voice came over the talkback and asked me if I would play one of Billy's guitars instead of my Martin. He said they were looking for a different sound. They couldn't see me, so I made a lot of noise like I was changing things around when all I did was reach in my pocket and get a different guitar pick. It was a lighter gauge guitar pick because Bremner liked really light strings. I hit the guitar with this different pick and they came back on the talkback and said "Yeah, that's a lot better." I never did tell them.

Whatever I've needed Little Sister to do, she's always done it. Like the small Martin parlor guitars, she sounds great when you fingerpick. The cool thing is, if you're flatpicking and start rockin' her, after a little while, the body gets this resonance and vibration going. Once you get that thing going, it just really rocks. It's like a little rock-and-roll box.

KEVIN WELCH is a songwriter whose work has been covered by such artists as Garth Brooks, Trisha Yearwood, the Highwaymen, Waylon Jennings, Solomon Burke, and Linda Ronstadt.

After leaving Oklahoma at seventeen and knocking around in different bands, he landed in Nashville, writing songs for Tree Publishing. That association lasted seventeen years.

His self-titled debut album was recorded in 1990; his ninth and most recent, *A Patch of Blue Sky*, came out in 2010. Welch has been nominated for various awards by the Americana Music Association and has toured internationally with Fats Kaplin and Kieran Kane. Recent tours have been with his son, roots rocker Dustin Welch.

He runs the Kevin Welch Songwriting Workshop for both aspiring and seasoned songwriters.

He lives near Austin, Texas.

# KELLY WILLIS

## SOMETHING THAT MATTERS

My first guitar was a little Takamine and I brought it to Austin with me in the late 1980s. At that time, I didn't play guitar, but I wanted to. I had moved to Austin to pursue music, and I was putting my second band together, Kelly Willis and Radio Ranch.

Playing guitar is not my passion. I'm a singer and I was the front person for the band. Singing is my passion, but I wanted to be self-sufficient. I really didn't want to depend on other people in order to have a gig. And that's the way it had been the first couple of years as a singer. So I started taking lessons from David Murray, an amazing guitar player in Austin. Playing the guitar brought me independence.

A year after moving to Austin and forming my band, I signed a record deal with Tony Brown of MCA Records in Nashville. The Gibson factory had just opened in that area and they invited Tony to take a tour. He was the big hotshot at MCA. He was also my producer, so he brought me along on the tour. At the end, they gave me a guitar, a J-180, which is the Everly Brothers model. It's black with the tortoise shell pick guards.

It was very percussive, but I loved it. That percussive sound fit the kind of rockabilly country stuff I was doing at the time. I took it out on the road and about a month after I got it, the bridge started to come loose. I sent it back, and Gibson sent me another one to use as a loaner while they fixed mine.

I immediately liked the loaner better. It looked exactly like the first guitar, but it felt different. It seemed like a better guitar. So I just told them to keep the first one. They weren't very happy about that.

That Everly Brothers guitar is a very sentimental guitar for me. At the time, I was only twenty and very shy. I was dealing with major label attention, creating music in a studio, doing photo shoots and interviews, and all kinds of stuff new to me. It was thrilling and, at the same time, terrifying because I had a social phobia. I think anyone will tell you it's really uncomfortable just to stand on stage and not have something to do with your hands. When I'm not playing guitar, sometimes I feel a little bit removed.

My Everly Brothers guitar was my companion through all that. I think of Radio Ranch when I look at that guitar. It takes me back to that time of traveling with the band in a modified fifteen-passenger van and playing nightclubs. There were five of us and our dog. Those guys were like my brothers. Back then, we had no following. It was my first national tour, and we were just introducing ourselves to people.

One of the best things that happened to me in the past few years has been working with my husband, Bruce Robison. We put together a four-piece band while we worked out the sound for our duo project. We had a stand-up bass, electric guitar, and Bruce and I played acoustic guitars. It was very intimate.

I told Bruce that I don't want to stand there with nothing to do. Whatever we do, I want my guitar playing to matter. That was the first time I had an important job on the guitar. I really had to know what I was doing. Everyone could hear my playing in the mix. It was an important part of our stage show, and I got a lot better because of that.

Camaraderie happens when you make music with your friends. I still feel so incredibly lucky to be making music and occasionally feeling relevant. Once in a while, to feel you're putting something out there that matters . . . it's an amazing feeling.

KELLY WILLIS is a singer and songwriter whose songs have often been described as new traditional or alternative country.

Born in Lawton, Oklahoma, and raised on the East Coast, Willis made her way to Texas with her first band, Kelly and the Fireballs. She met her future husband, musician Bruce Robison, after moving to Austin.

She has seven solo albums to her credit, the first released in 1990. Willis's most recent efforts are collaborations with Robison, including *Cheater's Game* (2013) and *Our Year* (2014). While she has toured with Robison as The Bruce and Kelly Show, she has recently turned her attention back to solo work.

Willis lives in Austin.

# JAMIE LIN WILSON

## ONE GUITAR FOR THE REST OF YOUR LIFE

My guitar is a gift. It was first a gift from a brother I am very close to, then from a craftsman who restored it.

My brother Michael is only eighteen months older than me. We grew up in the country and were each other's playmates. We had a common group of high school friends, attended the same university, and graduated in the same ceremony.

A week after that graduation, Michael attended one of my band's shows in our hometown. On his drive home, he fell asleep and struck another car from behind. A passenger in that car was killed. I was the first person he called.

He was not arrested that night, but he voluntarily took a blood test. The test showed his blood alcohol level was over the legal limit. He was charged with Intoxication Manslaughter, a second-degree felony punishable by a prison sentence of two to twenty years.

Michael decided he would not plead not guilty when it was obvious he had caused the accident. After mitigation, the district attorney offered a plea bargain of three years and Michael agreed. He asked the judge if he could wait to surrender until after my wedding. Roy and I moved our date from June back to December as the judge gave him until the new year.

This crushed our family, but it also made us stronger. We leaned on each other, and someone from the family visited Michael every weekend for those three years. After I realized he was going to go, I sat down to write a song. It came out in one piece. "Michael" was a therapeutic work.

He served his time in the Wallace Pack Unit in Navasota, Texas. I was in a band then called the Sidehill Gougers. Every time we drove through the area, we stopped at a radio station in Navasota. I'd write to Michael ahead of time and tell him the day and time we'd be on the air. He would get all his friends to put their headphones on and listen to us. Music got to be a big part of our communication in those three years.

He was determined not to let prison define him and within a week after his release, he was offered a job as a construction superintendent. As soon as he got his feet back on the ground, he asked me, "If you could have just one guitar for the rest of your life, what would you choose?" At the time, I was playing a blond Epiphone Jumbo. I showed him a picture of a Gibson J-200 with a sunburst.

He found the guitar and bought it for me new. That was in 2007. He had learned leather crafting in prison and had made a beautiful guitar strap, which I still use.

It's a really good guitar. Every person who plays it tells me how much magic it has.

In September 2012, I was eight months pregnant and I had a two-year-old, Joanie. I had just returned home from a long California tour with the Trishas. I had a writing appointment with Jason Eady that morning. I had to take Joanie to the babysitter and get a bunch of things done before he got to my place. My husband was helping me unload my car, and I noticed he leaned my guitar against the back. I remember thinking I should grab that and take it inside. I was putting Joanie and her things in the car and thinking about the writing session. I started the car and backed up.

I felt the car go over something and just stopped. I put my head on the steering wheel and thought, "Oh, no . . . no. I did not just do that."

The case was upside down. I unzipped the top and saw the neck was intact. The bridge wasn't touched and the headstock was fine. There were a few cracks down the front. Though it looked fine, I knew it wasn't. I zipped it up and put it on the porch.

My husband was working on the roof of the house next door. I walked over and said, "I just ran over my guitar." The words were barely coming out of my mouth. He couldn't understand me, so I said it again and then I started crying.

After Jason got there, I opened the case, picked it up slowly, and turned it. The sides were busted out, and the back had a huge hole in it. I still worked with him that day. I got out my Epiphone and we wrote the title track to his next record.

Later, I took the guitar to Tom Oatley in Austin. He does all my guitar maintenance. All the pieces were in the case because I never took them out. "If you can do anything with this," I told him. "I'll name my first son after you." All I wanted was to have it back, if for nothing else, to hang on my wall or give to my daughter someday. I had no more expectations, or even hope.

Tom said, "I'm not going to do anything with it unless you're going to play it onstage when I'm done."

I told him that I have a backup guitar. "Just work on it until it's done. Take your time."

Several times he was ready to give up, but he would set it aside and then go back to it. He put a new maple back on it and he glued together all the braces inside. He even put the broken shards of wood back in place. He told me, "I'll be finished with this by South by Southwest and you have to play it."

He kept it from September 2012 until March 2013.

I got it back right before the Trishas' first SXSW showcase at the Continental Club. I trusted Tom. I plugged it in and about halfway through the first song, I began to feel the magic. I was so overcome, I spaced on the lyrics. After the song, I explained to the crowd about my guitar and I told them that Tom works miracles.

He was there. "I cried," he said. "It sounded so good!"

It does. It sounds like an old guitar. It has a deeper, warmer, richer acoustic sound.

People tell me a guitar has to get banged around a little before it sounds good. It has to age and suffer a trauma before it starts sounding the right way. A lot of good songs came out of this guitar before the accident, but a lot of good songs have come out of it since. And I've played it at every gig since it was restored.

Tom says I'll never be able to sell it since it has a new back. Still, people say everything has a price, and I've been offered a lot of money for it.

This Gibson has already paid the price. It's not for sale.

Texan JAMIE LIN WILSON is a singer, songwriter, and musician and a veteran of two alternative country-roots bands.

From 2002 to 2009, she was a member of the Gougers, an alternative country band inspired by the work of Guy Clark and Townes Van Zandt, among others. The Gougers recorded four albums.

She then recorded a solo EP before joining three friends to form the Trishas, an all-female, alt-country band. The Trishas recorded an EP, toured nationally, and released a critically acclaimed album, *High, Wide and Handsome*, in 2012. Another solo album, *Holidays & Wedding Rings*, was released in 2015.

She has written or co-written songs that have been recorded by Jason Eady, Courtney Patton, Micky & the Motorcars, Owen Temple, Randy Rogers Band, and the Turnpike Troubadours.

Wilson lives in Texas.

# CAROLYN WONDERLAND

## PATTY THE BLUESHAWK

I had a couple of 50th Anniversary Telecasters. One I got at a guitar show—I can't remember if it was in Houston or Dallas—several years ago. It was the perfect deal and I dug it. It had Joe Barden pickups, so I dug it even more.

I have a Gibson Blueshawk. She's Patty the Blueshawk. Her namesake is the friend who gave her to me—Patrice Pike. We have been friends for years.

Several years ago, we were both touring. We had different routes, but we met up at Sturgis, South Dakota, at this biker rally. We had a show with Patrice.

Their trailer had been ripped off a week or two before. So they were playing on rented gear. You can't really rock out on rented gear because you're afraid you're gonna scratch it up.

But I had these two Telecasters. One was cleaner—I hadn't put the Joe Bardens on it yet. I gave that one to her because it was her birthday on one of the nights we were playing. I said, "Take it. Play it. Beat the hell out of it because it's a cheap guitar. You'll love it."

And when we came home, she gave me the Blueshawk. And that guitar had songs in it from the minute she gave it to me. I think every guitar has its own songs. The songs that are written on the Blueshawk are very different from the songs written on other guitars.

The Tele is pretty much just three positions. Throw some shit on it if you feel like being Albert Collins. Put it in this one position

if you feel like trying to be Roy Buchanan. And put it in this other position . . . well, that's about it on a Tele.

The Blueshawk has a lot of different sounds in any given room. You can go between these five positions. And there's a dial as well . . . it's not just tone.

She's a pretty far-out guitar. I had a lot of fun, and I got a little lost with her for a couple of months, just making weird noises. The Blueshawk is unique. She's got some cool pickups.

Every night is a different adventure with her. I recognized her personality instantly. The first night I brought her out it was like, "Okay, I can't use her for *these* songs . . . but for these *other* songs."

It's not as radical a difference as, say, between a Les Paul and a Tele. Patty kind of works all that ground in the middle. But she has these really dark things. She can be like an old rosewood Strat—she's got that kind of depth to her. And she has a warmer quality. The Blueshawk's got a lot of body without too much mid-range honk. It's pretty cool.

It worked out fine. Some people are blood sisters. Patrice and I are guitar sisters.

CAROLYN WONDERLAND is a singer, songwriter, multi-instrumentalist, and blues rocker from Houston, Texas.

She began performing as a teenager around her hometown and has developed a style incorporating elements of country and rock and roll. Her musical style, though, is rooted firmly in the blues.

She recorded her first album in 1993 with her band, the Imperial Monkeys. Her ninth, *Peace Meal*, was released in 2011. She has been honored numerous times by the Austin Music Awards and the Houston Press Music Awards.

Wonderland lives in Texas with her husband, writer and comedian A. Whitney Brown.

# ACKNOWLEDGMENTS

IN THE FALL OF 2007, I began collecting stories from professional guitarists about that one guitar that was most important to each of them. These stories were collected by simply asking and by referrals from fellow musicians.

The countless e-mails, interviews, photo shoots, and travel resulted in a monumental volume of work. I could not have done it without help from a lot of people.

The idea for this book stemmed from a conversation with Rick Oltman of Waterloo, Iowa. Early on, I relied on my brother, Paul Holley, to read my edited text. Later, Jeff Moravec, a friend from Minneapolis, stepped in. They each brought a perspective, a keen eye, and advice that proved invaluable.

The body of work I assembled after five years was brought to the attention of David Hamrick, director of the University of Texas Press. Dave shared my work with his editor-in-chief, Robert Devens. Robert embraced the premise, serving as my editor and sounding board. He pulled together a talented team composed of Lynne Chapman, Sally Furgeson, Sarah McGavick, and book designer Lindsay Starr.

Photo shoots in several cities followed. In Nashville, I was allowed to photograph at Gruhn Guitars, the Cannery Ballroom, the Ryman Auditorium, Starstruck Studios, and the City Winery.

In Austin, I arranged photo shoots at the Continental Club, Saxon Pub, Oatley's Guitar Garage, Spider House, Threadgill's, and El Mercado. With the help of Cindy Cashdollar and Deborah Fleming, I used Marcia Ball's home studio for a photo shoot. My work also took me to John T. Floore's Country Store in Helotes, the Hill Top Café in Cherry Spring, and Mission Concepción in San Antonio.

I photographed artists at the Newberry Opera House in Newberry, South Carolina; Kingston Mines and the Beverly Arts Center in Chicago; Tony Daigle's recording studio in Lafayette, Louisiana; Knuckleheads Saloon in Kansas City; and the White Theatre in Overland Park, Kansas.

Some artists graciously welcomed me to their home turf for their portraits. My thanks to John Leventhal, Rosanne Cash, G. E. Smith, Dave Alvin, Waddy Wachtel, Laurence Juber, Greg Leisz, Louie Pérez, Guy Clark, Bill Hullett, Tommy Emmanuel, Eliza Gilkyson, David Holt, Jack Lawrence, Dave Malone, Jorma Kaukonen, James Pennebaker, Redd Volkaert, Ray Benson, and Kevin Welch.

It was not unusual for an artist to suggest I interview other guitarists for this project. Casper Rawls, Webb Wilder, Cindy Cashdollar, Lisa Morales, Dan Dugmore, John Leventhal, Daniel Ivankovich, David Holt, Cornell Hurd, Rosie Flores, and Colin Gilmore all helped in this way.

I also owe thanks to Dan Rizzie, Dianne Scott, Matt Hessburg, Edward O'Day, Paul Babin, Joe Glaser, Chris Swope, Glen Tracy, Cash Edwards, Claire Armbruster, M. J. Mendell, Karol Walk, Tim Schumacher, and Mike Thompson.

When I needed photo retouching assistance, I turned to Michael Grevas and his first-rate skills with Adobe Photoshop.

None of this would have been possible without the encouragement and support of my wife, Patty, and my son, Michael. Patty was there to offer feedback when asked and encouragement when I stumbled. I am grateful.

This book is dedicated to the memory of Brad Moore.